100 LITERACY HOMEWORK ACTIVITIES

- Stand-alone homework sheets
- Fits with any programme
- Easy to use

YEAR 3

Scottish Primary 4

Chris Webster

ACKNOWLEDGEMENTS

Published by Scholastic Ltd,
Villiers House,
Clarendon Avenue,
Leamington Spa,
Warwickshire CV32 5PR

Printed by Bell & Bain Ltd, Glasgow

1 2 3 4 5 6 7 8 9   6 7 8 9 0

AUTHORS
Chris Webster

EDITORIAL
Sarah Snashall and Roanne Davis

DESIGN
Crystal Presentations Ltd

COVER DESIGN
Joy Monkhouse

ILLUSTRATOR
Theresa Tibbetts

British Library Cataloguing-in-Publication Data
A catalogue record for this book is available from the British Library.

ISBN 0-439-96586-1
ISBN 978-0439-96586-6

The publishers gratefully acknowledge permission to reproduce the following copyright material:

Egmont Children's Books for the use of extracts from *Storm* by Kevin Crossley-Holland © 1985, Kevin Crossley-Holland (1985, Heinemann Young Books).
Katherine Froman for the use of 'Friendly Warning' by Robert Froman from *Seeing Things* by Robert Froman © 1974, Robert Froman (1974, Thomas Y Cromwell Company, New York).
Johnson and Alcock for the use of an extract from *A Kind of Thief* by Vivien Alcock © 1991, Vivien Alcock (1991, Methuen Children's Books).
Laura Cecil Literary Agency and the James Reeves Estate for the use of 'Moths and Moonshine' by James Reeves from *Complete Poems for Children* by James Reeves © 1994, James Reeves (1994, Heinemann).
Brian Moses for the use of 'Whale' by Brian Moses from *Knock Down Ginger and other poems* by Brian Moses © 1994, Brian Moses (1994, Cambridge University Press).
Peters Fraser and Dunlop Group for the use of 'Dialogue between two large village women' by James Berry from *Caribbean Poetry Now* edited by Stewart Brown © 1984, James Berry (1984, Arnold Overseas).
Peters Fraser and Dunlop Group for the use of an extract from *The Sniff Stories* by Ian Whybrow © 1989, Ian Whybrow (1989, Bodley Head).
Peters Fraser and Dunlop for the use of 'I'm just going out for a moment' by Michael Rosen from *Wouldn't you like to know?* by Michael Rosen © 1977, Michael Rosen (1977, Andre Deutsch).
Saltkrakan AB for the use of an extract from *Emil gets into mischief* by Astrid Lindren © 1979, Astrid Lindgren (1979, Hamlyn).
Sony/ATV Music Limited for the use of the lyrics 'Eleanor Rigby' by John Lennon and Paul McCartney © 1966, Lennon and McCartney.
Walker Books for the use of an extract 'Hot Sleepysaurus' from *Our Sleepysaurus* by Martin Waddell, illustrated by Clive Scruton © 1988, Martin Waddell (1988, Walker Books).
Extracts from the National Literacy Strategy © Crown copyright. Reproduced under the terms of HMSO Guidance Note 8.

Every effort has been made to trace copyright holders and the publishers apologise for any omissions.

100 Literacy Homework Activities: Year 3

CONTENTS

Using the books

The activities in each book are organised by term, then by word-, sentence- and text-level focus and, finally, by specific National Literacy Strategy objective. Each of the 100 homework activities is comprised of at least one photocopiable page to send home. Each sheet provides instructions for the child and a brief note to the helper (be that a parent, grandparent, neighbour or sibling), stating simply and clearly its purpose and suggesting support and/ or a further challenge to offer the child. Every sheet is clearly marked with a W (word), S (sentence) or T (text) symbol to designate its main focus. (Please note that 'they', 'them', 'their' has sometimes been used in the helper and teachers' notes to refer to 'child'. This avoids the 'he or she' construction.)

Making the most of these resources

The best way to use these homework resources is to use them flexibly, integrating them with a sequence of literacy sessions over a number of days. Such an approach will also ensure that the needs of an individual, or groups of children, are met in different ways. Some of the homework sheets will be greatly enhanced by enlarging them to A3 size as this provides children with more space in which to write. Others, for example, the sets of story cards, lend themselves to being laminated for reuse.

Here are some ideas for different types of use:

Preparation

- Give a word- or sentence-level homework activity to prepare for a skills session later in the week. This allows the skill to be reviewed in less time, thus leaving more time for group activities.
- Give a text-level homework activity as a way of preparing for more detailed work on a particular type of text in a future literacy lesson.
- Give work on a particular short text as preparation for further work on that text, or a related text, in a future lesson.

Follow-up

- Give a word- or sentence-level homework activity as a follow-up to a literacy lesson to provide more practice in a particular skill.
- Give a text-level homework activity as a creative way of responding to work done in a literacy lesson.
- Use one of the many short texts as a follow-up to a study of a similar type of text in a lesson.

Reinforcement

- Give selected word- or sentence-level homework to specific children who need extra practice.
- Give a text-level homework activity to specific children to reinforce text-level work done in class.
- Use a short text with specific children to reinforce work done on similar texts.

Supporting your helpers

The importance of involving parents in homework is generally acknowledged. For this reason, as well as the 'Dear Helper' note on each homework sheet, there is also a homework diary sheet on page 128 which can be photocopied and sent home with the homework. Multiple copies of these can be filed or stapled together to make a longer-term homework record. For each activity, there is space to record its title, the date on which it was sent home and spaces for responses to the work from the helper, the child and the teacher. The homework diary is intended to encourage home-school links, so that parents and carers know what is being taught and can make informed comments about their child's progress. It is also worth writing to parents and helpers, or holding a meeting, to discuss their role. This could include an explanation of how they can support their children's homework, for example, by:

- providing a space where the child can concentrate and has the necessary resources to hand;
- becoming actively involved by interpreting instructions, helping with problems, sharing reading and participating in the paired activities where required.

Discuss with them how much time you expect the child to spend on the homework. If, after that time, a child is stuck, or has not finished, then suggest to the parent/helper that they should not force the child to continue. Ask them to write an explanation and the teacher will give extra help the next day. However, if children are succeeding at the task and need more time, this can be allowed – but bear in mind that children need a varied and balanced home life!

It is worth discussing with parents what is meant by 'help' as they should be careful that they do not go as far as doing the homework for the child. Legitimate help will include sharing the reading of texts, helping to clarify problems, discussing possible answers, etc., but it is important that the child is at some stage left to do his or her best. The teacher can then form an accurate assessment of the child's strengths and weaknesses and provide suitable follow-up work.

Using the activities with the All New 100 Literacy Hours series

A cross-referenced grid has been provided (on pages 5, 6 and 7) for those who wish to use these homework activities with the corresponding *All New 100 Literacy Hours* book. The grid suggests if and where a homework task might fit within the context of the appropriate *All New 100 Literacy Hours* unit and there may be more than one appropriate activity. Sometimes, the homework page could be used for a skills session in class and one of the resources from *All New 100 Literacy Hours* can be used for homework.

PAGE	HOMEWORK TITLE	USE AS A FOLLOW ON TO:	NLS OBJECTIVE LINK	LINK TO 100 LITERACY HOURS
28	**Adding –ing**	Looking at words ending in 'ing'	Y3 T1 W8	Unit 2 Hour 5
29	**A little snivel**	Looking at words ending in 'le' and el'	Y3 T1 W9	
30	**Prefix game**	Investigating prefixes	Y3 T1 W10	Unit 6 Hour 4
31	**Multi-purpose prefixes**	Creating new words by adding prefixes. Links with page 67	Y3 T1 W11	Unit 6 Hour 4
32	**Nice day out**	Substituting synonyms for high-frequency words	Y3 T1 W17	Unit 4 Hour 9
33	**Mash**	Writing dialogue. Links to pages 34, 36, 41–2, 48	Y3 T1 W19	Unit 2 Hour 3
34	**Karen's secret**	Investigating how punctuation helps the reader	Y3 T1 S2	Unit 2 Hour 1 Unit 3 Hour 4
35	**Verb tables**	Reinforcing verb tenses	Y3 T1 S4	Unit 2 Hour 5
36	**Hot Sleepysaurus**	Identifying speech marks. Links to pages 33, 34, 41–2, 48	Y3 T1 S7	Unit 2 Hour 1
37	**Capital letters in speech**	Looking at punctuation in dialogue	Y3 T1 S7	Unit 2 Hour 2/4
38	**Shopping game**	Punctuating lists	Y3 T1 S13	Unit 6 Hour 2
39	**Story Settings**	Focusing on story settings	Y3 T1 T1	Unit 1 Hour 1
40	**Picture the setting**	Creating story settings in own writing	Y3 T1 T1	Unit 1
41	**Presenting dialogue (1)**	Looking at how dialogue is presented in stories. Use alongside pages 33, 34, 36, 37, 42	Y3 T1 T2	Unit 2 Hour 1/2
42	**Presenting dialogue (2)**	Looking at how dialogue is written. Use alongside pages 33, 34, 36, 37, 41	Y3 T1 T2	Unit 2 Hour 1/2
43	**Schoolbot**	Writing own playscripts/follow up to improvisation	Y3 T1 T4	Unit 3
44	**Whale poems**	Focusing on poems. Links with pages 45, 46, 51–53	Y3 T1 T6	Unit 4 hour 4
45	**Comparing poems**	Comparing two poems on the same subject. Links to page 44, 46, 51–53	Y3 T1 T6	Unit 4
46	**I had a boat**	Comparing a range of poems. Links to pages 44, 45, 51–53	Y3 T1 T7	Unit 4 Hour 2/10
47	**Book review (1)**	Reading a story/expressing views	Y3 T1 T8	Unit 1
48	**Model dialogue**	Writing dialogue. Links to pages 33, 34, 36, 37, 41–42	Y3 T1 T10	Unit 2
49	**Once upon a time**	Preparing to write a story. Links to page 50	Y3 T1 T11	Unit 1 Hour 3/5
50	**Happily ever after**	Preparing to write a story. Links to page 50	Y3 T1 T11	Unit 1 Hour 3/5
51	**Homework poem**	Comparing and contrasting poems. Links to pages 44–6, 52 and 53	Y3 T1 T12	Unit 4
52	**Knock, knock**	Looking at poems. Links to pages 44–6, 51 and 53	Y3 T1 T12	Unit 4
53	**Shape up!**	Looking at poems. Links to pages 44-6, 51 and 52	Y3 T1 T13	Unit 4
54	**Bored boy**	Following up on improvised drama	Y3 T1 T14	Unit 3 Hour 2/3
55	**Puppy problem**	Preparing to write a story/looking at paragraphing	Y3 T1 T15	Unit 1 Hour 3–5
56	**Fiction and non-fiction**	Investigating differences between fiction and non-fiction	Y3 T1 T16	Unit 5 Hour 3
57	**Fact or fiction?**	Investigating differences between fiction and non-fiction	Y3 T1 T16	Unit 5 Hour 3
58	**Crocodiles**	Differences between fiction and non-fiction	Y3 T1 T17	Unit 5
59	**King Arthur**	Comparing non-fiction texts	Y3 T1 T19	Unit 6 Hour 1
60	**Hurricane**	Preparing to write a summary	Y3 T1 T20	Unit 6 Hour 1
61	**Turbo trouble**	Writing simple reports	Y3 T1 T22	Unit 6 Hour 4/5

PAGE	HOMEWORK TITLE	USE AS A FOLLOW ON TO:	NLS OBJECTIVE LINK	LINK TO 100 LITERACY HOURS
62	**Adding -er and -est**	Understanding how words change when 'er' and 'est' are added	Y3 T2 W8	
63	**Adding -s**	Changing the spelling of nouns when 's' is added	Y3 T2 W9	Unit 2 Hour 1
64	**The silence of 'lamb'**	Investigating the spelling of words with silent letters	Y3 T2 W10	Unit 3 Hour 1
65	**A pair of trousers**	Revising/reinforcing the terms singular and plural. Use as an alternative to 63 for less able children	Y3 T2 W11	Unit 2 Hour 1
66	**The suffix kit**	Reading texts with words with suffixes ('ful', 'less', 'ly')	Y3 T2 W13	
67	**Multi-purpose suffixes**	Word-building using suffixes	Y3 T2 W14	
68	**Don't do it**	Using the apostrophe to spell shortened forms of words	Y3 T2 W15	
69	**Excel scientific instruments**	Preparing to read a non-fiction text with difficult vocabulary	Y3 T2 W18	Unit 4 Hour 2
70	**CD collection**	Work on alphabetical order	Y3 T2 W23	
71	**An alphabet of my dislikes**	Looking at alphabetical order/language patterns for free-verse poems	Y3 T2 W23	
72	**Opposite story**	Extending vocabulary by looking at opposites	Y3 T2 W24	Unit 1 Hour 6
73	**Think of an adjective**	Experimenting with different adjectives	Y3 T2 S2	Unit 1 Hour 7
74	**Singular to plural**	Practising spellings of plural forms	Y3 T2 S4	Unit 2 Hour 1
75	**A gaggle of geese**	Looking at collective nouns	Y3 T2 S4	
76	**How commas help**	Preparing for work on commas	Y3 T2 S6	Unit 1 Hour 1
77	**Schoolbot's poem**	Focusing on capital letters	Y3 T2 S8	
78	**Let's get personal**	Understanding the differences between verbs in first, second and third person	Y3 T2 S10	
79	**Let's agree**	Reinforcing grammatical agreement in written work	Y3 T2 S11	
80	**Typical story language**	Reading and writing traditional tales. (See pages 73, 81, 84, 87, 88)	Y3 T2 T1	Unit 2 Hour 1
81	**The choosing**	Reading and writing traditional tales	Y3 T2 T2	Unit 1 Hour 1 Unit 2 Hour 1
82	**Emil**	Studying a main character during shared reading	Y3 T2 T3	Unit 1 Hour 4/5
83	**Dialogue Between Two Large Village Women**	Looking at performance poetry or drama	Y3 T2 T4	Unit 1 Hour 1/Unit 3
84	**Plot cards**	Reading and writing traditional tales	Y3 T2 T6	Unit 2 Hour 2-4
85	**Story game**	Summarising the plot of a novel or story	Y3 T2 T7	Unit 2 Hour 4 Unit 1 Hour 3/8
86	**Character card**	Studying characters from a story	Y3 T2 T8	Unit 1 Hour 7
87	**How the elephant got a long trunk**	Reading or writing myths, legends or traditional tales	Y3 T2 T9	Unit 1 Hour 2 Unit 2 Hour 5
88	**The sequel game**	Reading or writing traditional tales	Y3 T2 T10	Unit 2 Hour 3
89	**Sequel planner**	Reading or writing traditional tales. Alternative to page 88	Y3 T2 T10	Unit 2 Hour 3–5
90	**Why?**	Exploring pattern/repetition in poems	Y3 T2 T11	Unit 3 Hour 5
91	**Instructions**	Looking at instructional texts	Y3 T2 T12	Unit 4 Hour 1
92	**New mini-system**	Looking at instructional texts	Y3 T2 T14	Unit 4 Hour 1/6/7
93	**How to make a book**	Preparing to write instructions	Y3 T2 T15	Unit 4 Hour 1/6/8/9
94	**How to make a recording**	Preparing to write instructions	Y3 T2 T16	Unit 4 Hour 5/7/9/10
95	**Notes**	Practising note-taking	Y3 T2 T17	Unit 4 Hour 2–5

PAGE	HOMEWORK TITLE	USE AS A FOLLOW ON TO:	NLS OBJECTIVE LINK	LINK TO 100 LITERACY HOURS
96	**Words within words**	Spelling (Finding short words within longer ones)	Y3 T3 W8	
97	**Non-stick**	Word-building/spelling prefixes	Y3 T3 W9	
98	**Pirate talk**	Collecting synonyms for 'said'	Y3 T3 W13	Unit 1 Hour 3/4 Unit 2 Hour 8
99	**A wet blanket**	Looking at idioms in a shared text	Y3 T3 W16	
100	**Provide a pronoun**	Using pronouns to improve paragraph cohesion	Y3 T3 S2	Unit 1 Hour 4
101	**Roboteach**	Looking at personal pronouns and possessive pronouns	Y3 T3 S2	Unit 1 Hour 2/4
102	**In agreement**	Ensuring grammatical agreement of pronouns and verbs	Y3 T3 S3	
103	**Willa's baby**	Preparing to write/redrafting a story with dialogue	Y3 T3 S4	Unit 1 Hour 3/ Unit 2 Hour 1/4/8
104	**Grace Darling**	Using conjunctions to improve writing	Y3 T3 S5	Unit 4 Hour 2
105	**Time sequence**	Writing or redrafting narrative/recount using connectives	Y3 T3 S6	Unit 5 Hour 1/2
106	**The Ant and the Grasshopper**	Sequencing or organising stories into paragraphs	Y3 T3 T1	Unit 2 Hour 3 Unit 5 Hour 1/2
107	**Will-o'-the-Wykes and bogles**	Discussing how language is used to create a mood in a story	Y3 T3 T2	Unit 2 Hour 2/6
108	**First or third?**	Thinking about first or third person before writing a story	Y3 T3 T3	Unit 1 Hour 1
109	**Stranger than fiction?**	Planning to write a story	Y3 T3 T4	Unit 2 Hour 2
110	**Pirates**	Comparing character portrayal in fiction and non-fiction	Y3 T3 T5	Unit 1 Hour 5
111	**Sandwich fillings**	Investigating humour in poetry	Y3 T3 T6	Unit 3
112	**Eleanor Rigby**	Studying songs, ballads or oral poetry	Y3 T3 T7	Unit 3
113	**Comparing poems**	Comparing poems by the same writer. Could be used to compare two poems by Allan Ahlberg in 100 Literacy Hours	Y3 T3 T8	Unit 1 Unit 3
114	**Robin Hood**	Developing longer stories based on a known plot	Y3 T3 T10	Unit 2 Hour 2
115	**Sleeping Beauty**	Retelling a story from another character's point of view	Y3 T3 T12	Unit 1 Hour 1
116	**Improve a story**	Writing extended stories	Y3 T3 T13	Unit 2 Hour 7
117	**Book review (2)**	Reading and discussing a story	Y3 T3 T14	Unit 4 Hour 3
118	**Moths and Moonshine**	Looking at alliteration in rhymes and poems	Y3 T3 T15	Unit 3 Hour 4
119	**Bank letter**	Investigating the conventions of letter writing	Y3 T3 T16	Unit 5 Hour 4
120	**Seaside index**	Preparing for research using features of non-fiction texts	Y3 T3 T17	Unit 6 Hour 5
121	**Be a librarian**	Using the library for research	Y3 T3 T18	Unit 6 Hour 2/3
122	**Letter to an author**	Practising letter-writing skills	Y3 T3 T20	Unit 5 Hour 5 Unit 4 Hour 5
123	**John Keats**	Publishing writing through ICT	Y3 T3 T21	Unit 3 Hour 2 Unit 6 Hour 1/3
124	**Guy Fawkes**	Recounting an event as a letter	Y3 T3 T22	Unit 5 Hour 3
125	**Letters**	Organising writing into paragraphs	Y3 T3 T23	Unit 5 Hour 2/4/5
126	**Book organisation**	Working on alphabetical order; looking at indexes	Y3 T3 T24	Unit 6 Hour 1/5
127	**Crabs**	Summarising and rewriting the key points from a piece of text	Y3 T3 T26	Unit 5 Hour 1

Teachers' notes

TERM 1

p28 ADDING -ING

Objective
Understand how spellings of verbs alter when *-ing* is added. (Y3, T1, W8)

Lesson context
Use as a follow-up to any text that provides several examples of words ending in *-ing*.

Setting the homework
Revise the rules for adding *-ing* by using the explanation on the homework sheet.

Differentiation
Less able children may need to be reminded of the terminology (*verb, vowel, consonant*) and the difference between long and short vowels.

Back at school
Displaying the page on an , go over the words while the children check their own sheets.

p29 A LITTLE SNIVEL

Objective
Investigate and learn to use the spelling pattern *-le*. (Y3, T1, W9)

Lesson context
Use as a follow-up to any text that provides several examples of words ending in *-le* and *-el*.

Setting the homework
Explain that both *-le* and *-le* endings usually have the same sound – 'l'. This means that each spelling has to be learned – there are no easy rules!

Differentiation
Less able children should work on the first column only. Demonstrate how to say the printed part of the word and follow it immediately with an 'l' sound.

Back at school
Go over the words while the children check their own sheets. Children should make a list of words they got wrong for further LOOK, SAY, COVER, WRITE, CHECK practice.

p30 PREFIX GAME

Objective
Recognise and spell common prefixes and understand how these influence word meanings. (Y3, T1, W10)

Lesson context
Use as a follow-up to any text that provides examples of words with the prefixes *un-*, *de-*, *dis-* and *re-*, or as part of a series of lessons on word-building.

Setting the homework
Define *prefix*: a word-part added to the beginning of a word to change its meaning. Explain how to play the prefix game using the instructions on the homework sheet.

Differentiation
Ask more able children to think about how prefixes change the meanings of words.

Back at school
Write the correct matches of prefixes and words on the board in a brainstorming session with children. Talk about how the prefixes change the meanings of the words.

p31 MULTI-PURPOSE PREFIXES

Objective
Use knowledge of prefixes to generate new words from root words. (Y3, T1, W11)

Lesson context
Use with any lesson where the focus is on new words generated by the use of prefixes. See also page 67, 'Multi-purpose suffixes', which is a companion to this homework sheet with a focus on suffixes.

Setting the homework
Explain that many prefixes are linked to particular words and cannot be used flexibly. For example, we say '*un*happy' and '*dis*agree', but it is wrong to say '*dis*happy' and '*un*agree'. However, there are some prefixes which can be used very flexibly to create new words, and indeed, many recent new words have been formed from them, for example '*super*market'. Go over the three examples on the homework sheet with the children. Encourage them to combine one of the prefixes with any word they can think of, then to say what their new word means. For example, 'cyber' + 'desk' = 'cyberdesk: a special desk with a built-in computer'.

Back at school
Enjoy sharing the new words and definitions. Create a class dictionary of new words. Research the use of these prefixes in the real world, for example 'megastore'. Ask the class to write a story set in the future using as many of these new words as possible.

p32 NICE DAY OUT

Objective
Generate synonyms for high-frequency words. (Y3, T1, W17)

Lesson context
Use when redrafting a piece of writing or preparing for writing.

Setting the homework
Remind the children that a *synonym* is a word that has a similar meaning to another. There is nothing wrong with the words *big, little, like, good, nice* and *nasty,* but they are used too often and, with a little more thought, more descriptive words can be found. The homework sheet lists some synonyms of these words, but there are many more and the children should be encouraged to think of their own if they can.

Differentiation
Less able children could be asked to work with fewer words, eg *big* and *little* only.

Back at school
Display the text on an OHP and discuss the alternative words that the children chose. Get the children to apply this skill to a piece of their own writing which is ready to be redrafted, or to a story that is about to be written. It is a good idea to make a game of it and ban these six words for a few weeks.

p33 MASH

Objective
Develop common vocabulary for introducing and concluding dialogue. (Y3, T1, W19)

Lesson context
Preparing, writing or redrafting a story. This sheet can also be used along with pages 34, 36, 37, 41–2 and 48 as part of a series of lessons on writing dialogue.

Setting the homework
Remind the children that dialogue can be brought to life by using synonyms of 'said'. This gives the text variety and tells us more about the feelings of the speaker. This is not a one-for-one cloze procedure: there are more synonyms than gaps, and synonyms can be used twice.

Differentiation
More able children should be encouraged to think of synonyms of their own.

Back at school
Brainstorm the most effective synonym for each gap. Get the children to apply the skill to their own story-writing.

p34 KAREN'S SECRET

Objective
Take account of grammar and punctuation, eg sentences, speech marks, exclamation marks and commas to mark pauses, when reading aloud. (Y3, T1, S2)

Lesson context
This homework is useful as a follow-up to a lesson on any aspect of punctuation because it demonstrates how punctuation helps the reader. It can also be used with pages 33, 36, 37, 41–2 and 48 as part of a series on writing dialogue.

Setting the homework
Explain that punctuation not only makes clear which parts of the text are narration and which are dialogue, but it also gives guidance on intonation. Ask the children to look out particularly for question marks and exclamation marks.

Differentiation
Less able children will need the support of their helper.

Back at school
Ask a group of volunteers to read the passage aloud. Remind the children of the importance of accurate punctuation in their own writing.

p35 VERB TABLES

Objective
Use verb tenses with increasing accuracy. (Y3, T1, S4)

Lesson context
Use as a reinforcement of class work on verbs.

Setting the homework
Go over the explanation on the sheet. Revise the terms *singular* and *plural* and revise (or teach) the terms *first, second* and *third* person. It is worth spending some time on this, because it lays a foundation for more advanced work on verbs in Year 4.

Differentiation
Less able children may struggle with the concept of person, but they should be able to complete the verb tables by using their common sense. More able children could be asked to write verb tables for the simple past tense of these verbs.

Back at school
Go over the two verb tables completed by the children and, where appropriate, give them more verb tables to complete.

p36 HOT SLEEPYSAURUS

Objective
Identify speech marks in reading. (Y3, T1, S7)

Lesson context
Use when redrafting a story, or preparing to write a story. This sheet can also be used along with pages 33, 34, 37, 41–2 and 48 as part of a series of lessons on writing dialogue.

Setting the homework
Revise speech marks with the children. It is worth pointing out that speech marks can occur as single or double quote marks. Emphasise that they are used before and after *words actually spoken*.

Differentiation
Identifying speech marks is one of the first steps in learning to punctuate dialogue. This homework is therefore most suited to less able children. More able children could be given pages 33, 34, 37, 41–2 or 48, as appropriate.

Back at school
Ask for a small group of volunteers to share reading the passage aloud. To do this well, they will have to take account of the speech marks.

p37 CAPITAL LETTERS IN SPEECH

Objective
Use capital letters to mark the start of direct speech. (Y3, T1, S7)

Lesson context
Use when redrafting a story, or preparing to write a story. This sheet can also be used with pages 33, 34, 36, 41–2 and 48 as part of a series of lessons on writing dialogue.

Setting the homework
Remind the children of the uses of capital letters that they have covered so far, such as for the personal pronoun 'I', at the start of a sentence, for the names of people and places and for headings and titles. Revise or introduce the use of capital letters in dialogue by using the explanation on the sheet.

Differentiation
This skill should be introduced when a child has both mastered the basic uses of capital letters and learned how to use speech marks. Less able children who have not mastered these skills should be given work on these instead.

Back at school
Display the sheet on an OHP to go over the uses of capital letters. Follow up the homework by asking the children to write a story with dialogue.

p38 SHOPPING GAME

Objective
Use commas to separate items in a list. (Y3, T1, S13)

Lesson context
This is suitable with any shared or guided reading session that focuses on the punctuation of lists.

Setting the homework
Explain how to set out the lists using the example given at the bottom of sheet. In particular, emphasise that the last item is joined by using 'and', not by using a comma.

Back at school
Share some of the lists, then ask the children to write stories or descriptions that include lists, eg 'My birthday', 'Christmas' or 'Packing for a holiday'.

p39 STORY SETTINGS

Objective
Compare a range of story settings and select words and phrases that describe scenes. (Y3, T1, T1)

Lesson context
Use with a shared or guided reading session where the focus is on story settings, or a session that prepares for writing a story.

Setting the homework
Explain that writers cannot describe every detail in a scene; it would take up too much space, and would be boring. Instead, they select a few key details and describe them carefully. Ask the children to look for the key details of the scenes on the sheet. Tell them to underline or highlight the words and phrases that describe these details.

Back at school
Discuss each of the settings and share ideas about what brings each one to life. You could ask the children to choose one of these settings – or one of their own – to use as the basis for a story.

p40 PICTURE THE SETTING

Objective
Compare a range of story settings and select words and phrases that describe scenes. (Y3, T1, T1)

Lesson context
This homework can be used as a follow-up to the previous one. Here, the emphasis is on writing rather than reading.

Setting the homework
Ask the children to choose one of the picture settings and to describe it in detail, using the present tense, eg 'The market place *is* filled with little stalls...' Encourage them to expand on the detail that can be seen in the pictures.

Differentiation
More able children could choose to write about more than one picture.

Back at school
As a class, share the descriptions that the children have written. Ask the children to plan a story around the setting they have written about. A good way to begin the story is simply with the description of the setting, making only one change – putting it into the past (or 'story-telling') tense. For those children who chose to write about more than one setting, the others can be introduced later on in the story.

p41 PRESENTING DIALOGUE (1)

Objective
Understand how dialogue is presented in stories and how paragraphing is used to organise dialogue. (Y3, T1, T2)

Lesson context
Use in the context of preparing to write or redrafting a story. This sheet can also be used with pages 33, 34, 36, 37, 42 and 48 as part of a series of lessons on writing dialogue.

Setting the homework
Revise the use of speech marks, then emphasise the point that each new speaker requires a new line.

Differentiation
This skill should be introduced only when a child has learned how to use speech marks. Children who have not mastered this skill should be given work on this instead. Alternatively, work on playscripts (see pages 43 and 54) will lay a good foundation for this stage.

Back at school
Apply this skill in the context of story writing.

p42 PRESENTING DIALOGUE (2)

Objective
Understand how dialogue is presented in stories and how paragraphing is used to organise dialogue. (Y3, T1, T2)

Lesson context
Use in the context of preparing to write or redrafting a story. This sheet can also be used with pages 33, 34, 36, 37, 41 and 48 as part of a series of lessons on writing dialogue.

Setting the homework
Briefly revise the previous steps covered, eg the use of speech marks, the use of other punctuation and starting a new line for each new speaker. Then go over the explanation on the sheet. Note: by the time children get to this stage, there is a great deal of punctuation and setting out to remember, so do not expect them to master this all at once!

Differentiation
This skill should be introduced only when a child has mastered the previous steps (see above). Children who have not mastered these skills should be given work on those instead.

Back at school
Look at lots of examples of dialogue in published books. Apply the skill in the context of story writing.

p43 SCHOOLBOT

Objective
Read, prepare and present playscripts. (Y3, T1, T4)

Lesson context
This homework is good preparation for further improvised drama on the same subject, or for writing own playscripts as a follow-up to improvisation. See also page 54, which is on the same subject and is a specific preparation for writing a playscript.

Setting the homework
Explain to the children that this scene sets up a situation that could be developed into a play. Spend a few moments going over the conventions of drama scripts: scene descriptions in present tense, brief directions in brackets, no speech marks for dialogue and no reporting clauses (eg 'said Schoolbot').

Back at school
Organise the children into groups of four to six. In each group, one person should play the part of the teacher, one Schoolbot, and the others should play the children in the class. Ask the groups to begin by reading the script, then to improvise more scenes. Emphasise that they need to make up names for the characters of the children and to give each one a worthwhile part to play. The lesson might conclude with one or two of the groups acting out a scene from their play to the rest of the class.

p44 WHALE POEMS

Objective
Read aloud and recite poems, comparing different views of the same subject. (Y3, T1, T6)

Lesson context
Use in the context of a series of lessons on poetry, along with pages 45, 46 and 51–53.

Setting the homework
This homework compares a traditional ballad on the excitement and profit of whaling, with a modern poem about the tragedy of hunting whales to extinction. Explain to the children that in the past hunters threw harpoons by hand at the whales to kill them. Ask the children to look at how each message is expressed, particularly at the words and phrases used. Note that this homework only requires children to read and discuss with their helper. Page 45 can be used if a written response is desired.

Differentiation
Less able children should be able to notice the difference in the way the whale is treated and the verse form of the two poems.

Back at school
Read and discuss these two poems as a class. Note that the first one is an extract from a longer poem.

p45 COMPARING POEMS

Objective
Read aloud and recite poems, comparing different views of the same subject. (Y3, T1, T6)

Lesson context
Use in the context of a series of lessons on poetry, along with pages 44, 46 and 51–53. This sheet should be used as a follow-up to reading two poems on the same subject in class. Copies of the poems should be available for the children to take home (page 44, 'Whale poems', could be used).

Setting the homework
It would be a good idea to enlarge this sheet to A3 size to allow more room for writing. Alternatively, the children could use the homework sheet as a prompt and write on a separate sheet of paper. The best way to help the children with this sheet is to ensure that class discussion of the poems has followed the format of the sheet. This sheet should only be used without class discussion if the children have previously discussed other poems in the same way.

Differentiation
Less able children should be encouraged to make notes during the class discussion.

Back at school
Discuss the children's ideas and opinions about the poems.

p46 I HAD A BOAT

Objective
Distinguish between rhyming and non-rhyming poetry and comment on the impact of layout. (Y3, T1, T7)

Lesson context
Use in the context of a series of lessons on poetry, along with pages 44, 45 and 51–53.

Setting the homework
Ensure the children understand that *rhyme* occurs when words end with the same sound. Explain that *non-rhyming* poems are often called *free verse* poems.

Differentiation
Less able children should just identify which is the rhyming and which is the non-rhyming poem. More able children could also be asked to colour-code the rhymes in the rhyming poem and to try to explain the effect of the line breaks on the way the non-rhyming poem is read.

Back at school
Ask the children to look through a poetry anthology that contains rhyming and non-rhyming poems and to pick out several examples of each.

p47 BOOK REVIEW (1)

Objective
Express views about a story, identifying specific words and phrases to support their viewpoint. (Y3, T1, T8)

Lesson context
This homework is a good follow-up to individual reading (shared or guided reading of stories should lead to more detailed study).

Setting the homework
It would be a good idea to enlarge this sheet to A3 size to allow more room for writing. Alternatively, the children could use the homework sheet as a prompt and write on a separate sheet of paper. Encourage the children to find words and phrases to quote in support of their ideas.

Differentiation
More able children should be encouraged to write on separate sheets of paper so that they can expand their ideas more fully.

Back at school
Share some of the book reviews. Compile them into a class anthology that the children can browse through to get ideas for reading.

p48 MODEL DIALOGUE

Objective
Using reading as a model, write own passages of dialogue. (Y3, T1, T10)

Lesson context
Use when redrafting or preparing to write a story. This sheet can also be used with pages 33, 34, 36, 37 and 41–2 as part of a series on writing dialogue.

Setting the homework
Take the children very carefully though the example on the sheet and explain how the model relates to it.

Differentiation
This homework is not intended for every child; it has been designed for those children who are struggling to set out dialogue in paragraphs, eg those who did not attempt or did not do well on page 42, 'Presenting dialogue (2)'.

Back at school
Encourage the children to use the dialogue model in a story. They should note that it can be used several times.

p49 ONCE UPON A TIME

Objective
Investigate and collect sentences/phrases for story openings. (Y3, T1, T11)

Lesson context
Use as part of the preparation for writing a story. Note that this sheet can be used by itself or with page 50, 'Happily ever after' (see 'Back at school' notes for page 50). The endings on page 50 match the openings on this sheet.

Setting the homework
Ask the children to talk about each of the openings with their helper with a particular focus on what kind of story each opening might lead in to.

Differentiation
Less able children could concentrate on the first task only.

Back at school
Discuss the openings, then ask the children to choose one to develop into a story during shared or guided writing.

p50 HAPPILY EVER AFTER

Objective
Investigate and collect sentences/phrases for story endings. (Y3, T1, T11)

Lesson context
Use as part of the preparation for writing a story. Note that this sheet can be used by itself or with page 49, 'Once upon a time' (see 'Back at school' below).

Setting the homework
Ask the children to talk about each of the endings with their helper, with a particular focus on what kind of story might have led up to them.

Differentiation
Less able children could concentrate on the first task only.

Back at school
Discuss the endings, then ask the children to choose one and write a story to go with it during shared or guided writing. Alternatively, the children could cut up the openings from page 49 and the endings from page 50, shuffle them and then try to match them up. More able children could combine them at random, and try to write a story that fits!

p51 HOMEWORK POEM

Objective
Use repetitive phrases in order to write poems. (Y3, T1, T12)

Lesson context
Use in the context of a series of lessons on poetry, along with pages 44–6, 52 and 53.

Setting the homework
Explain that poetry is language made into patterns. The most well-known pattern is rhyme, but repetition can also be very effective and is much easier to write. Ask the children to read the poem, and then add more excuses to finish it off.

Differentiation
Less able children could omit the second task (writing another poem).

Back at school
Share the excuses written by the children. Combine the excuses into a new whole-class poem. When several excuses have been jotted on the board, discuss which order to write them in. The class might decide, for example, to end with the funniest or most ridiculous.

p52 KNOCK, KNOCK

Objective
Design simple patterns with words in order to write poems. (Y3, T1, T12)

Lesson context
Use in the context of a series of lessons on poetry, along with pages 44–6, 51 and 53. Note that 'Knock, knock' jokes also have other educational uses: they are a good way to reinforce the concept of a new line for each speaker in dialogue.

Setting the homework
Explain that 'Knock, knock' jokes are like little free-verse poems because they all follow a set pattern. Encourage the children to enjoy reading the jokes and to write some of their own.

Back at school
Share the children's new 'Knock, knock' jokes. A good follow-up would be to investigate free-verse poetry that is based on patterns, eg repetition (see pages 51 and 90).

p53 SHAPE UP!

Objective
Invent calligrams and a range of shape poems, selecting appropriate words and careful presentation. Build up class collections. (Y3, T1, T13)

Lesson context
Use in the context of a series of lessons on poetry, along with pages 44–6, 51 and 52.

Setting the homework
Go over the definitions on the sheet, ensuring the children understand the difference between a calligram and a shape poem.

Back at school
Compile a class collection of calligrams and shape poems.

p54 BORED BOY

Objective
Write simple playscripts based on own reading and oral work. (Y3, T1, T14)

Lesson context
This homework makes a good follow-up to improvised drama as it provides a model for scriptwriting. Note: the homework on page 43, 'Schoolbot', could be used for an earlier linked homework, perhaps as a preparation for the improvised drama session.

Setting the homework
Spend a few moments going over the conventions of drama scripts. Ask the children to compare the story text with the playscript 'starter' at the bottom of the page.

Differentiation
More able children should be able to complete the playscript. Less able children could just compare the two versions of the story.

Back at school
The children should apply the skill to writing an extended drama script. Ask each group to write a script of their improvised drama. If the subject matter of the drama was planned in advance, each scene could be edited together to form a full-length play. Try to find a performance opportunity for the play, eg in an assembly or to another class.

p55 PUPPY PROBLEM

Objective
Begin to organise stories into paragraphs. (Y3, T1, T15)

Lesson context
This homework is good preparation for writing a story, or can be used to reinforce work on paragraphs.

Setting the homework
Explain the basic rules of paragraphing (indent first line of each paragraph after the first one; begin a new paragraph for each big step forward in the story). Explain that the template on the homework sheet will help the children to apply these rules.

Differentiation
More able children should be encouraged to develop the template and write a longer story with more paragraphs.

Back at school
Encourage the children to apply the rules of paragraphing without the support of a template. This can be done in stages, eg by first suggesting a paragraph plan and leaving the children to set out the paragraphs correctly and then leaving them to work out their own paragraph plans.

p56 FICTION AND NON-FICTION

Objective
Understand the distinction between fact and fiction. (Y3, T1, T16)

Lesson context
This homework goes well with a study of basic library classification. It also reinforces work on alphabetical order.

Setting the homework
Ensure that the children understand the terms: *fiction* – a made up story (a true story is usually biography or history); *non-fiction* – any type of writing that is not a story (eg history, science, diaries, advertisements, reports); and *fact* – something which is true.

Differentiation
This sheet is a simpler alternative to page 57, 'Fact or fiction?' Both sheets can be used at the same time, with less able children using this sheet and the more able using page 57.

Back at school
Discuss the sorting exercise, particularly how the children classified *Operation Titanic* and *The Story of Queen Victoria*. A good follow-up would be a visit to the library to see how books are classified.

p57 FACT OR FICTION?

Objective
Understand the distinction between fact and fiction. (Y3, T1, T16)

Lesson context
This homework goes well with a study of basic library classification and with any work on different kinds of texts.

Setting the homework
Ensure that the children understand the terms *fiction, non-fiction* and *fact* (see above). Explain that the task is to sort the openings into fact and fiction. Some are easy, but others are intended to be thought-provoking. For example, the last one sounds like a fact, but does Fushun really exist?

Differentiation
This sheet is a more difficult alternative to page 56, 'Fiction and non-fiction'. Both sheets can be used at the same time, with less able children using page 56 and the more able using this sheet.

Back at school
Discuss the sorting exercise, with a particular focus on the thought-provoking lines. Some of the points to bring out are:

- A text can sound factual because of the way it is written, but could be deliberately false or could be fiction.
- A story can be written about a factual event. Is it then fact or fiction? The answer depends on the style in which it is written and who it is written for.
- It is difficult to classify texts about people's beliefs (eg belief in God, belief in Atlantis) as fact or fiction. This is where the term *non-fiction* is so helpful.

p58 CROCODILES

Objective
Notice differences in the style and structure of fiction and non-fiction writing. (Y3, T1, T17)

Lesson context
Use with pages 56 and 57 as part of a study of fact, fiction and non-fiction.

Setting the homework
Revise the terms *fiction* and *non-fiction* (see above). Explain that the extracts on the sheet are very short, but that there is just enough text to be able to answer the questions. Ask the children to discuss the questions with their helper and to write their answers on the back of the page.

Differentiation
For less able children, the sheet could be simplified by deleting the 'Fiction' and 'Non-fiction' headings and the questions. The children could then be asked to say which passage is fiction and which is non-fiction.

Back at school
Discuss the questions at the bottom of the sheet. Find and compare other examples of fiction and non-fiction passages on the same subject.

p59 KING ARTHUR

Objective
Compare a variety of information texts including ICT-based sources. (Y3, T1, T19)

Lesson context
Use as part of a study of the range of non-fiction texts.

Setting the homework
Discuss the different ways in which information is available today, eg books, videos, CDs, the Internet and so on. Explain that the homework sheet focuses on a web page and an information book page. Stress that the sheet only shows the beginning of each text. The children should draw on their own experience of using both books and the Internet to compare the two different types of sources.

Back at school
Share ideas with the whole class and, if possible, set up an investigation using real websites and books.

p60 HURRICANE

Objective
Read information passages and identify main points. (Y3, T1, T20)

Lesson context
Use as a first step in learning how to write summaries.

Setting the homework
Explain that the text contains about 15 points, however, they are not all equally important. The task is to pick out four of the most important points.

Differentiation
More able children could be asked to rewrite their four main points into a paragraph of connected prose.

Back at school
Discuss the points chosen. Some flexibility should be allowed – what makes a 'main point' is sometimes a matter of interpretation. The first of the following points, plus any other three (though not 4 *and* 5, as they are similar points) would be a good answer:

1. A hurricane is a very strong wind.
2. Hurricanes are about 250 to 450km across.
3. The strength of hurricanes is measured on a scale of 1 to 5.
4. The strongest hurricane of the century was Hurricane Gilbert.
5. In Britain, the worst hurricane was in 1987.
6. Modern weather forecasts can give warning of hurricanes.

p61 TURBO TROUBLE

Objective
Write simple non-chronological reports from known information. (Y3, T1, T22)

Lesson context
As part of a series of lessons on non-fiction or report writing.

Setting the homework
Tell the children that they must look very carefully at the picture to write their notes. Encourage them to be specific when writing about the fault, eg instead of 'cracked window', they should be encouraged to write something like 'large crack in the window of the front passenger door.'

Differentiation
Less able children should do the first task only.

Back at school
Discuss the faults that were found on the car. Who managed to find them all? Compare versions of the report.

TERM 2

p62 ADDING -ER AND -EST

Objective
Understand how words change when *-er* and *-est* are added. (Y3, T2, W8)

Lesson context
This homework lays a foundation for the study of comparative and superlative adjectives in Year 4.

Setting the homework
Revise the rules on the homework sheet to ensure the children understand them.

Differentiation
For more able children, the words 'Comparative' and 'Superlative' could be given as the headings of the last two columns.

Back at school
Quickly go over the exercise, then discuss how the meaning of a word changes when *-er* and *-est* are added.

p63 ADDING -S

Objective
Investigate and identify basic rules for changing the spelling of nouns when *-s* is added. (Y3, T2, W9)

Lesson context
The homework is intended as a follow-up to a lesson on basic rules for plurals of nouns. It does not include exceptions to rules, or rules for adding s for contraction or possession.

Setting the homework
Revise the terms *singular* and *plural* before explaining the sorting exercise.

Differentiation
More able children could be given a set of cards with words written in the *singular*. They would then have to apply the rules and write the plural form on the back of the cards as they sort them. Alternatively, they could be given page 74, 'Singular to plural'.

Back at school
Quickly go over the sorting exercise, then give the children a short list of singular words for them to pluralise by applying the four rules they investigated for homework.

p64 THE SILENCE OF 'LAMB'

Objective
Investigate, spell and read words with silent letters. (Y3, T2, W10)

Lesson context
Use as a follow-up to a text containing several examples of silent letters or as part of a spelling programme.

Setting the homework
Encourage the children to work hard on this list, which contains many words that cause spelling problems and examples of most of the common patterns of silent letters.

Differentiation
Less able children could work on simpler lists containing more examples of common patterns of silent letters (see, for example, the lists on page 11 of the National Literacy Strategy Spelling Bank).

Back at school
Ask the children to test each other in pairs. Revisit this list on a number of future occasions.

p65 A PAIR OF TROUSERS

Objective
Use the terms *singular* and *plural* appropriately. (Y3, T2, W11)

Lesson context
Use after revision and consolidation of the terms *singular* and *plural*.

Setting the homework
Revise the terms *singular* and *plural* and brainstorm some examples in class.

Differentiation
This homework consolidates skills covered much earlier (see Year 2, Term 1) and is therefore best used with individuals or groups who are still struggling to grasp these concepts. Children of average ability and above might work on page 74, 'Singular to plural' instead (though this sheet would provide a sufficient challenge if the children were asked to make all singulars plural and all plurals singular).

Back at school
Go over the exercise, particularly the more difficult words, eg 'a pair of shoes' – two objects, but the word *pair* makes them grammatically singular; 'sheep' and 'fish' – the same in both singular and plural so should appear in both columns; 'trousers' – one object, but grammatically plural; the addition of a *pair of* would make it singular; 'flock' – this is a collective noun; it refers to a group of animals, but is grammatically singular (see page 74, 'Singular to plural').

p66 THE SUFFIX KIT

Objective
Recognise and spell common suffixes and understand how these influence word meanings. (Y3, T2, W13).

Lesson context
Use as a follow-up to any text that provides several examples of words with the suffixes *-ful, -less* and *-ly,* or as part of a series of lessons on word building (see also pages 28, 30, 31, 62, 63, 67 and 97).

Setting the homework
Define *suffix*: a suffix is a word-part that can be added to the end of another word to change its meaning. Explain to the children that they should cut out the cards and experiment with different combinations, writing down every combination that works. Emphasise that they need to use the information given at the bottom of the page. It is worth going over this in class.

Differentiation
More able children could be asked to think of more examples of words that use these suffixes.

Back at school
Find out who generated the greatest number of correct combinations. Share any new words that were found.

p67 MULTI-PURPOSE SUFFIXES

Objective
Use knowledge of suffixes to generate new words. (Y3, T2, W14)

Lesson context
This homework can be part of a series of lessons on word building (see pages 28, 30, 31, 62, 63, 66 and 97).

Setting the homework
Explain that many suffixes are linked to particular words and cannot be used flexibly. For example, we say 'beautiful' but not 'happiful'. However, there are some suffixes which can be used very flexibly to create new words, eg 'readathon', which uses the suffix *-athon,* from 'marathon', meaning a long event requiring lots of stamina. Ten of the commonest of these multi-purpose suffixes are listed on the homework sheet. Go over the three examples with the children and encourage them to combine the suffixes with any word they can think of, then to say what it means, eg 'gorilla-speak – a special language made up of grunts'.

Back at school
Create a class dictionary of new words. Research the use of these suffixes in the real world, eg 'user-friendly'.

p68 DON'T DO IT

Objective
Use the apostrophe to spell shortened forms of words, eg 'don't', 'can't'. (Y3, T2, W15)

Lesson context
Use as a preparation for writing dialogue in informal writing, eg diaries and personal letters.

Setting the homework
Ask the children to study the pairs of cards before they cut them up. After the matching exercise, they should write out the shortened forms to check that they can spell the words correctly and put the apostrophe in the right place.

Back at school
Check the application of this skill in everyday writing.

p69 EXCEL SCIENTIFIC INSTRUMENTS

Objective
Infer the meaning of unknown words from context. (Y3, T2, W18)

Lesson context
This homework is a good preparation for reading any text with difficult vocabulary, particularly scientific and technical terms.

Setting the homework
Explain that most of the words we know have been learned by inferring (figuring out) their meanings from the context (the situation in which we hear or read the words). We should have the confidence to continue learning words in this way. Explain to the children that if they read the text carefully, they will find that most of the difficult words are explained.

Differentiation
More able children may already know most of these words. They could be given a more challenging passage instead. Similarly, less able children could be given a passage with simpler words to deduce.

Back at school
Definitions are one thing, but for the children to really understand these words, it will help to see photographs of the actual instruments. If possible, make suitable reference books or CD-ROMs available.

p70 CD COLLECTION

Objective
Organise words or information alphabetically using the first two letters. (Y3, T2, W23)

Lesson context
Link with any lesson where the work has focused on alphabetical order. The homework could be used as a preparation for developing reference skills.

Setting the homework
Explain that information is often arranged in alphabetical order. When the children have sorted the CDs by composer, they should paste them in alphabetical order onto another sheet.

Differentiation
More able children can be given two copies of the sheet and asked to use the second copy to sort the CDs by title. This is more difficult as they will have to go beyond the second letter when sorting.

Back at school
Quickly go over the sorting exercise, then apply the skill to an educational context, such as making an index for a piece of non-fiction writing.

p71 AN ALPHABET OF MY DISLIKES

Objective
Organise words alphabetically. (Y3, T2, W23)

Lesson context
Use as a follow-up to work on either alphabetical order or on language patterns for simple, free-verse poems.

Setting the homework
Explain that the alphabet has been used as a pattern for poems for hundreds of years. Encourage the children to finish off the poem, expressing their genuine dislikes – though they will sometimes have to make up a dislike to fit a particular letter.

Differentiation
Less able children could be allowed to miss out any letters they find difficult (eg Q, X, Y or Z) or to limit the letters to those in their name.

Back at school
Enjoy sharing the alphabet poems. If the focus of the lesson is alphabetical order rather than poetry, ask the children to exchange poems, cut them up into sentences, shuffle them and reassemble them in alphabetical order. They will also enjoy mixing up each other's dislikes and making new, random alphabet poems!

p72 OPPOSITE STORY

Objective
Explore opposites. (Y3, T2, W24)

Lesson context
Exploring opposites is an excellent way to build up vocabulary. Thus, this homework is a good follow up to any work on vocabulary extension.

Setting the homework
Brainstorm some opposites (such as 'damp/dry', 'upper/lower', 'doctor/patient'). Then explain that the homework is to make a whole story opposite. Emphasise how important it is to choose opposites that *fit the story* (eg 'Naughty boy!' or 'Lazy boy!' reads better than the exact opposite, 'Bad boy!').

Back at school
Go over the opposites that the children have chosen. This could be followed up by asking the children to write their own story, which could then give to a partner to make opposite.

p73 THINK OF AN ADJECTIVE

Objective
Experiment with deleting and substituting adjectives. (Y3, T2, S2)

Lesson context
Use as a follow-up to any lesson on adjectives. This sheet can also be used as one of a series of lessons on traditional tales (see pages 80, 81, 84, 87 and 88).

Setting the homework
Revise the terms *noun* and *adjective*. Explain that the task is to write adjectives to bring out the difference between pairs of pictures of the same thing. Encourage the children to try out different adjectives before choosing one to write in the gap.

Differentiation
More able children could be asked to make up their own pairs. They could also experiment with using two adjectives: 'A/an *adjective, adjective* noun'.

Back at school
Share the adjectives and discuss which are the most effective. To prepare for story-writing, ask the children to visualise scenes, objects and characters and to choose adjectives carefully.

p74 SINGULAR TO PLURAL

Objective
Extend knowledge of plurals through transforming sentences from singular to plural. (Y3, T2, S4)

Lesson context
Use as part of a series of lessons on singular and plural or as a specific homework for groups of children who need more practice in this area.

Setting the homework
Revise the terms *singular* and *plural*. It will also be helpful to revise the terms *noun, verb* and *pronoun*. However, explain that this exercise can be done by using common sense (ie the children's internalised knowledge of the grammatical structure of the English language).

Differentiation
This homework is best suited to children of average ability and above. Less able children should do more basic work on singular and plural (see page 63, 'Adding -s').

Back at school
Go over the sentences. If you have time, do a similar exercise in reverse by making plural sentences singular.

p75 A GAGGLE OF GEESE

Objective
Understand the term *collective noun* and collect examples – experiment with inventing other collective nouns. (Y3, T2, S4)

Lesson context
Use this homework as part of the study of nouns or plurals. It would also be a relevant way to follow up any text in which a number of collective nouns are used.

Setting the homework
Revise the terms *noun* and *collective noun*. The children should note that collective nouns are *singular*, even though they refer to a *group* of things. Go through the example on the sheet.

Differentiation
Delete the harder examples for less able children. Encourage more able children to invent their own (eg 'a grumble of grannies').

Back at school
Go over the correct pairings and share any new collective nouns that the children have invented.

p76 HOW COMMAS HELP

Objective
Note where commas occur in reading and discuss their functions in helping the reader. (Y3, T2, S6)

Lesson context
This homework is a good preparation for further work on the specific uses on the comma. It can also be used as part of a programme designed to improve reading aloud.

Setting the homework
Remind the children of some of the main uses of commas. When reading aloud, a comma usually indicates a slight pause. Explain to the children that they should prepare the text by highlighting the commas and then should read it aloud to someone. After the reading, they should discuss how the commas helped their reading.

Back at school
Move on to more specific uses of the comma and/or other punctuation marks that help the reader.

p77 SCHOOLBOT'S POEM

Objective
Understand uses of capitalisation from reading. (Y3, T2, S8)

Lesson context
This sheet focuses on capitalisation to begin names and places, direct speech, brand names and lines of poetry. The skill of capitalisation needs constant revisiting. It is particularly effective to do this before writing, or as part of the redrafting process.

Setting the homework
Revise the main uses of capital letters. Explain the sorting task and emphasise that those words that recur need only be written down once.

Differentiation
The more able could be asked to continue the passage using capital letters correctly. Ask them: 'How will Schoolbot finish his poem? What will Karen think of it?

Back at school
Go over the capitalised words that have been sorted into columns. Apply the skill to writing as soon as possible.

p78 LET'S GET PERSONAL

Objective
Understand the differences between verbs in the first, second and third person through relating to different types of text. (Y3, T2, S10)

Lesson context
This homework complements work on verbs (eg page 35, 'Verb tables') or work on point of view in texts.

Setting the homework
Define the term *personal pronoun*: pronouns that are used in place of a person or thing. Go over the table on the sheet to ensure that the children understand it. Explain the homework task to the children and encourage them to find other texts to identify the person they are written in. (Note: verbs can also indicate person, eg an -s ending indicates third person singular, as in 'she walks'.)

Differentiation
Less able children could limit their work to the sheet only, leaving average and above average ability children to find additional texts.

Back at school
Discuss the person of each text on the sheet and how it was identified, then ask the children to share the other texts they found.

p79 LET'S AGREE

Objective
Understand the need for grammatical agreement in speech and writing. (Y3, T2, S11)

Lesson context
This homework is best suited for use by individuals or groups who make repeated errors of agreement. Note that errors of agreement have two main causes: one is local dialect/slang forms and the other is sentences with complex subjects that are not easy to identify as singular or plural. This homework addresses both these in a simple way and is limited to the verb 'to be'.

Setting the homework
Revise the terms at the top of the sheet. The first four sentences (at least in areas where the local dialect is not far removed from standard English) should not be problematic. However, for the remaining four, encourage the children to think carefully about whether the subject is singular or plural before choosing the singular or plural verb. Explain that it is often the second part of the subject that causes the confusion. For example, in the sentence 'All but Sam are going to the concert', the phrase 'but Sam' makes us think of one person and therefore singular, but if we go back to the beginning, we can see that the subject is really 'All' and therefore plural. Encourage the children who have difficulties with this to write out a verb table for the verb 'to be' in full for both the present and past tense. (See page 35 for examples of verb tables.)

Differentiation
Less able children could do the first four examples only. They could also be asked to write out a verb table for the present tense of 'to be'.

Back at school
Go over the exercise, and follow up by checking how well the children are applying what they have learned to their written work.

p80 TYPICAL STORY LANGUAGE

Objective
Investigate the styles and voices of traditional story language. (Y3, T2, T1)

Lesson context
This homework should be used as one of a series of lessons based on reading and writing of traditional tales (see also pages 73, 81, 84, 87 and 88). In particular, this homework, which focuses on style, would be a good follow-up to planning a story (see page 84, 'Plot cards').

Setting the homework
Explain to the children that an important feature of traditional tales is the language in which they are written. This language reflects the fact that the stories were usually passed on by word of mouth for hundreds of years. Encourage the children to relate the example phrases to stories they have read and to think of or collect more examples and add them to the list. They should then try to use some of the words and phrases in a story of their own.

Differentiation
Less able children could limit their work to writing examples rather than tackling their own story.

Back at school
Share any new examples of traditional story language and some of the stories.

p81 THE CHOOSING

Objective
Identify typical story themes. (Y3, T2, T2)

Lesson context
This homework would be a useful preparatory study for a series of lessons based on the reading and writing of traditional tales (see also pages 73, 80, 84, 87 and 88).

Setting the homework
The children should be familiar with the term *theme,* although you may wish to revise it: a theme is a main idea expressed in a story (eg the triumph of good over evil), as opposed to *plot,* which is what happens in the story.

Differentiation
Theme is an abstract concept which less able children will probably not be able to grasp at this stage. However, they can enjoy and discuss the story at a more concrete level, and should be able to answer the questions.

Back at school
Discuss the answers to the questions. Ask the children to share any situations they have experienced where they had to make choices. Read a number of other short fairy and folk tales and try to identify the themes.

p82 EMIL

Objective
Identify and discuss main characters. (Y3, T2, T3)

Lesson context
Use as a preparation for, or as a follow-up to, studying a main character in a shared reading text.

Setting the homework
Explain to the children that this extract introduces us to Emil. In order to get enough information for a full character study we would have to find out what he does and how he changes throughout the story.

Back at school
Discuss the children's answers to the questions. The third question could be used as a basis for the children to write their own adventures for Emil.

p83 DIALOGUE BETWEEN TWO LARGE VILLAGE WOMEN

Objective
Choose and prepare poems for performance, identifying appropriate expression, tone, volume and use of voices and other sounds. (Y3, T2, T4)

Lesson context
Use as a follow-up or preparation to a lesson or series of lessons on performance poetry or drama.

Setting the homework
Explain that part of the fun of performing this poem is to pronounce the words phonetically (ie as they are spelled) and hear an echo of the West Indian accent.

Differentiation
Less able children may find so many phonetically spelled words difficult to follow. They could work on a simpler performance poem, such as 'I'm just going out for a moment' on page 90. The more able, and those who wish to, could improvise the scene that the women are talking about, or a new scene with these two characters.

Back at school
Ask for volunteers to perform the poem and any newly made-up scenes.

p84 PLOT CARDS

Objective
Plan main points as a structure for story writing. (Y3, T2, T6)

Lesson context
Use as part of a series of lessons based on the reading and writing of traditional tales (see also pages 73, 80, 81, 87 and 88). Note that these cards can be used alongside the 'Myth-maker Cards' in *100 Literacy Hours: Year 3* (pages 91–94).

Setting the homework
Explain that many fairy tales are developed from a small number of basic plots, six of which are given on the sheet. Ask the children to discuss these plots with their helpers and to elaborate them by adding other ideas. Finally, they should choose one to write up into a detailed story plan.

Differentiation
By outcome. Less able children can follow the plots in a straightforward way. More able children should be encouraged to elaborate the plots and/or borrow from other plots.

Back at school
Share and discuss story plots, then begin the first draft of the stories.

p85 STORY GAME

Objective
Describe and sequence key incidents in a variety of ways. (Y3, T2, T7)

Lesson context
This homework is a good follow-up to the reading of a novel or story. It is similar to writing a plot summary – but more fun.

Setting the homework
The children will need to take a copy of the story home. If this is not possible, provide a summary sheet for them to work from. Make sure that the story lends itself to this kind of treatment. Most stories with a linear plot will work well. If possible, show the children a 'worked example'. This could be a good example from another class, or one you have prepared yourself. It is a good idea to enlarge the homework sheet to A3 size.

Differentiation
More able children could be encouraged to elaborate on the basic idea by adding in ideas from other board games they know about (eg 'Chance' cards).

Back at school
Share and discuss the games. The children will enjoy playing each other's games. If different groups of children have written about different books, the games may well stimulate an interest in further reading.

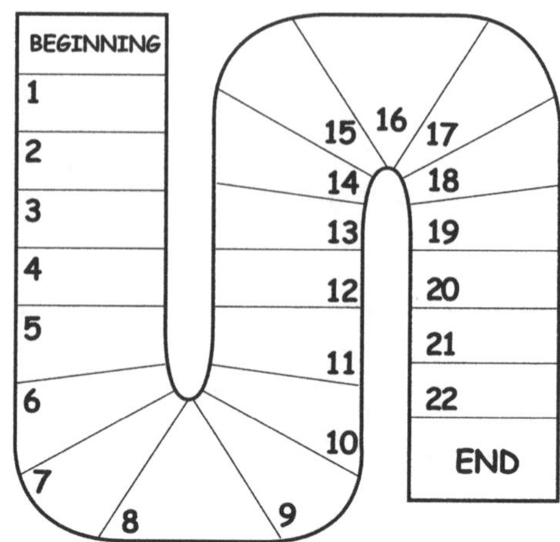

p86 CHARACTER CARD

Objective
Write portraits of characters, using story text to describe behaviour and characteristics. (Y3, T2, T8)

Lesson context
Shared or guided reading of a story where the focus is on character study.

Setting the homework
Ask the children to use the template (enlarged to A3 size if possible) to write about one of the main characters in a story that has been read and studied in class. Note that they will need to take the text home with them. If this is not possible, provide them with a written summary of the text and some notes and quotes – or get the children to do this in a lesson.

Differentiation
More able children should be encouraged to write more extensive portraits.

Back at school
Share ideas about the main characters.

p87 HOW THE ELEPHANT GOT A LONG TRUNK

Objective
Write a story plan for own myth using story theme from reading. (Y3, T2, T9)

Lesson context
Use as part of a study of myths, legends and traditional tales (see also pages 73, 80, 81, 84 and 88).

Setting the homework
Remind the children that myths often try to explain something we don't understand or how something came to be. Explain to the children that they should use the myth on the sheet, which explains how elephants got their long trunks, as a model for a similar myth of their own. Some ideas are given at the bottom of the page to help them, but they should be encouraged to come up with their own ideas if appropriate.

Back at school
Discuss the myth of the elephant's trunk. Ask the children: 'Is it a good explanation? Why did people long ago make up such myths?' Share the myths the children have written.

p88 THE SEQUEL GAME

Objective
Write alternative sequels to traditional stories. (Y3, T2, T10)

Lesson context
Use as part of a series of lessons based on the reading and writing of traditional tales (see also pages 73, 80, 81, 84 and 87).

Setting the homework
Define the term *sequel*: a sequel is a follow-on story that uses some of the same characters and settings. Ensure that the children are familiar with the basic stories featured on the sheet. Adapt the sheet if necessary to include more familiar titles.

Differentiation
The only obstacle to planning a sequel is lack of knowledge of the characters and settings of the original. Ensure that all the children are able to participate by adapting the sheet appropriately.

Back at school
Share plans for the sequels. These could then be written up and edited into a class book of traditional-story sequels.

p89 SEQUEL PLANNER

Objective
Write alternative sequels to traditional stories. (Y3, T2, T10)

Lesson context
This sheet can be used as an alternative to page 88, 'The sequel game', when a sequel to a particular text is required.

Setting the homework
Ideally, the children should take the texts home. However, if this is not possible, the children could make notes on the story on a separate sheet or in the 'Story' column of the sheet. The notes in the 'Story' column should be used as a basis to brainstorm ideas for the 'Sequel' column.

Back at school
Share ideas for sequels, then begin the first drafts.

p90 WHY?

Objective
Write new or extended verses for performance based on models of poetry read. (Y3, T2, T11)

Lesson context
Use as a follow-up to a lesson or series of lessons on poetry, particularly a lesson that explores patterns of repetition. See also page 51, 'Homework poem', which also focuses on repetition in poetry.

Setting the homework
Explain that patterns of repetition are often used instead of rhyme, especially in modern poetry. Ask the children first to add a few extra verses to the poem (a verse in this case being a statement followed by 'Why?') and then to try a whole new 'Why?' poem.

Back at school
Ask for volunteers to perform their poems in pairs.

p91 INSTRUCTIONS

Objective
Identify the different purposes of instructional texts. (Y3, T2, T12)

Lesson context
Use along with pages 92–94 as part of a series of lessons on instructional texts.

Setting the homework
Ask the children to read each text and say what its purpose is. Emphasise that an important part of the homework is finding more examples in the categories of recipes, route-finders, timetables, plans, rules and instructions. Suggest some places for the children to look.

Back at school
Prepare a notice-board or section of wall with headings for the six types of instructional text identified under 'Setting the homework' and ask the children to sort the instructions they have found and pin them up under the appropriate heading.

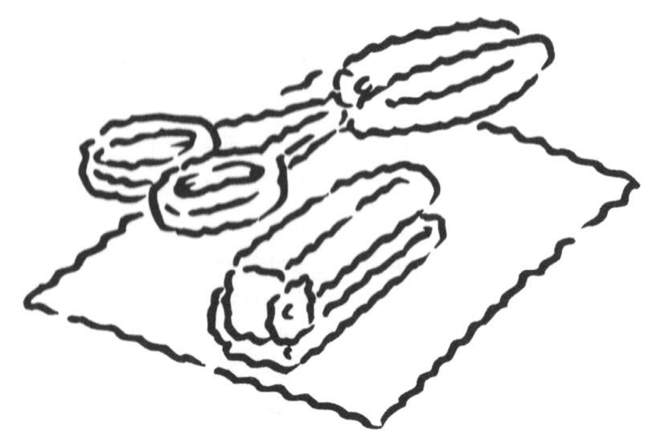

p92 NEW MINI-SYSTEM

Objective
Explore how written instructions are organised. (Y3, T2, T14)

Lesson context
Use along with pages 91, 93 and 94 as part of a series of lessons on instructional texts.

Setting the homework
Explain that written instructions use a wide range of features to make them as clear and helpful as possible. These include: lists, numbered points, diagrams with arrows, bullet points and keys. Ask the children to find examples in the instructions on the homework sheet. Encourage them to find examples of real instructions at home and highlight them (with their helper's permission) in the same way.

Differentiation
Some of the language on the sheet is difficult (though not essential to the task). It would therefore be helpful to explain the following to some children: 'hazard', 'retro', 'amplifier', 'teak-effect', 'antenna', 'Dolby B' (a system which reduces hiss on tape), 'trademark' and 'licensing'.

Back at school
Apply the same skill to examples of real instructions brought in by the children. Use these instructions as a model for writing an instruction manual for a product. This will work best if a real purpose can be found, such as for a product made in a design and technology lesson.

p93 HOW TO MAKE A BOOK

Objective
Read and follow simple instructions. (Y3, T2, T15)

Lesson context
The process of following instructions is the best preparation for writing instructions as it demonstrates the importance of clarity. See also pages 91, 92 and 94.

Setting the homework
It may be a good idea to give out sheets of A4 blank paper as this will not be available in every home. Explain that, if a stapler is not available, the children should leave out the staple and bring in the folded pages to be stapled in school. Finally, the children might be interested to know that this form of paper folding is used in the making of hardback books, and that, in the 18th and 19th centuries, readers had to cut the folds themselves.

Differentiation
More able children might like to experiment with making more of these foldings and stitching them together.

Back at school
Discuss the helpfulness of the instructions and examine the final products. It would be a good idea to use these miniature books for writing in.

p94 HOW TO MAKE A RECORDING

Objective
Write instructions. (Y3, T2, T16)

Lesson context
This homework would make a very good follow-up to page 93 as the instructions on that sheet could be used as a model. See also pages 91 and 92.

Setting the homework
Talk about how a recording is made using a cassette recorder. Most children will be familiar with this process, but the discussion will be a valuable reminder. It is also a good idea to refer to a model of how instructions are written (eg page 93, 'How to make a book'). Explain to the children that the numbers on the homework sheet are meant as a guide; they can add more or use bullet points instead if they prefer.

Back at school
Share some of the instructions. Check that the children have included all the important steps.

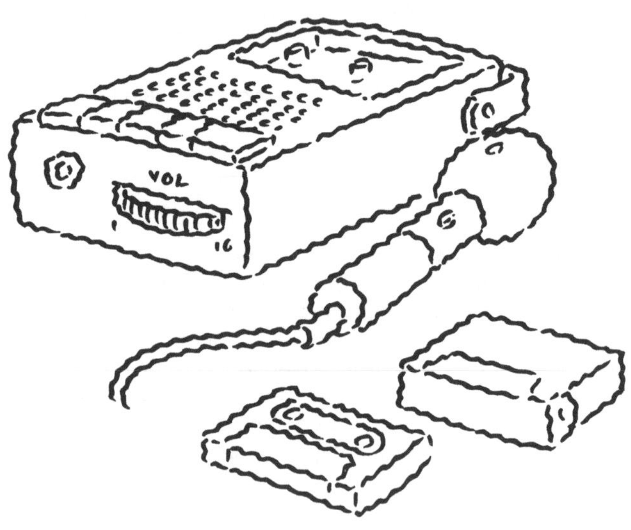

p95 NOTES

Objective
Make clear notes, discussing the purpose of note-making and looking at simple examples. (Y3, T2, T17).

Lesson context
A shared or guided writing session where the focus is on note-making. The homework task provides skills practice in preparation for applying the skill for a real purpose, eg research for a history lesson.

Setting the homework
Ask the children to compare the example encyclopedia entry with the notes very carefully. They will see that the notes are brief, that abbreviations have been used and that only the main points have been included. They should remember this to make similar notes on the next encyclopedia entry.

Differentiation
This exercise can be extended for more able children, by giving them longer or more difficult extracts on the same subject.

Back at school
The note-making exercise could be extended as suggested above, or the skill could be applied to research for another subject.

p96 WORDS WITHIN WORDS

Objective
Identify short words within longer words. (Y3, T3, W8)

Lesson context
Use as a follow-up to any lesson on spelling.

Setting the homework
Explain the game to the children by going over the rules on the sheet and writing an example on the board, such as 'blackcurrant – black, currant, lack, rant, ran, ant, an'.

Back at school
Go over some of the words on the cards. Give the children some additional words to work on.

p97 NON-STICK

Objective
Recognise and spell the prefixes *non-*, *ex-*, *co* and *anti-*. (Y3, T3, W9)

Lesson context
This homework can be part of a series of lessons on word building (see pages 28, 30, 31, 62, 63, 66 and 67). Alternatively, it could be used as part of a series of lessons on the development of the English language.

Setting the homework
Note that the prefixes *non-*, *ex-*, *co-* and *anti-* have been chosen (using only one meaning of *ex-*: former) as these are the prefixes most often used to coin new words.

Back at school
Share the new words. An interesting follow-up would be to ask children to sketch their new product (eg an *anti-tangle* shampoo) and write an advertisement or instruction manual for it.

p98 PIRATE TALK

Objective
Collect synonyms that will be useful in writing dialogue. (Y3, T3, W13)

Lesson context
This homework is intended as an extension of page 33, 'Mash', which deals with the commoner synonyms of 'said'. Both homeworks are a good preparation for writing a story with dialogue or redrafting a story.

Setting the homework
Revise the term *synonym*. Explain that a well-chosen synonym of 'said' can tell us a great deal about the feelings of the character speaking.

Differentiation
This sheet is appropriate for children who know and can use the synonyms of 'said' on page 33. Those who have not mastered these synonyms should be given more work on them instead.

Back at school
Compare the experiments with substituting synonyms in the passage. Sum up by saying that well-written dialogue will include synonyms in the reporting clause (the 'said' part of the dialogue) when appropriate, but that they should not be used all the time. Encourage the children to apply the skill to writing dialogue in stories.

p99 A WET BLANKET

Objective
Investigate common expressions. (Y3, T3, W16)

Lesson context
This homework is a good follow-up to shared or guided reading of any text that contains several idioms.

Setting the homework
Explain to the children that our language includes many common expressions (sometimes called *idioms*) which can be quite mystifying until you know them. Encourage the children to guess the meaning of any expressions that they do not know before asking their helper.

Differentiation
Most children will need help from an adult.

Back at school
Share the definitions of the common expressions and write on the board all the other common expressions that children found. Children could explore common expressions further by writing a story in which the characters use several common expressions in their speech.

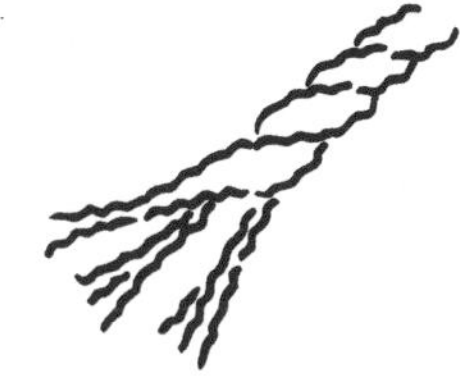

p100 PROVIDE A PRONOUN

Objective
Substitute pronouns for common and proper nouns. (Y3, T3, S2)

Lesson context
This homework is a good way of helping children to improve paragraph cohesion by the appropriate use of pronouns. It is therefore a good preparation for writing or can be used as part of the redrafting process.

Setting the homework
Revise the term *pronoun*. This sheet focuses on personal pronouns.

Differentiation
Most children should be able to do this exercise, though the less able could concentrate on just the first five examples, which use only two sentences.

Back at school
Quickly go over the exercise, then ask children to look at their own and each other's work to see if they have any sentences that are as repetitive as the examples on the sheet.

p101 ROBOTEACH

Objective
Distinguish personal pronouns and possessive pronouns. (Y3, T3, S2)

Lesson context
This homework takes page 100, 'Provide a pronoun', a step further by including both personal pronouns and possessive pronouns in the context of a whole passage rather than just a few sentences. It should be used to reinforce a lesson in which the distinction is taught.

Setting the homework
Revise the term *pronoun*. Revise personal pronouns and introduce possessive pronouns (which show that someone owns or possesses something). Explain that the text gives an extreme example of how repetitive writing sounds when pronouns are not used. The children should choose appropriate pronouns to replace the words in italic – note that it is not intended that all the pronouns listed should be used and some will need to be used more than once.

Differentiation
Children who struggle with personal pronouns should do more work on pronouns in pairs of sentences (see page 100).

Back at school
Briefly go over the exercise. Ask the children to look at their own writing in the same way. Are there any places when it would sound better to use a pronoun?

p102 IN AGREEMENT

Objective
Ensure grammatical agreement of pronouns and verbs in standard English. (Y3, T3, S3)

Lesson context
This homework can be used for individual or groups of children who consistently make errors of agreement. This is often a particular problem in areas where there is a strong local dialect. Work on verb tables (see page 35) is a valuable preliminary to this homework, as writing out a verb table can not only lead children to the correct answer, it can show them *why* it is correct.

Setting the homework
It is very important that children understand that these are the grammatical rules of *standard English*. There are many other varieties of English, such as regional and ethnic dialects. These have their own validity in their own context, but everybody needs to master standard English. Revise the terms *pronoun, verb, person* and *number,* and recap on how to write a verb table. Point out that writing verb tables will help to sort out any problems.

Differentiation
Sentences 1 to 4 contain some obvious mistakes of agreement of the kind often found in dialect or slang. Some children would benefit from doing these four sentences only, and perhaps being given another four similar sentences. Sentences 5 to 8 have the kind of complexity that can easily lead to confusion about agreement.

Back at school
Quickly go through the exercise. Be prepared to revise this skill, particularly for strong dialect speakers.

p103 WILLA'S BABY

Objective
Use speech marks and other dialogue punctuation appropriately. (Y3, T3, S4)

Lesson context,
Use as a preparation for writing a story with dialogue or at the redrafting stage. See also pages 33, 34, 36, 37, 41–42 and 48, all of which deal with different aspects of writing and punctuating dialogue.

Setting the homework
Explain that the highlighting exercise focuses attention on the speech marks and other punctuation. This will then be used as a model for their own writing.

Differentiation
There is a lot of punctuation to cope with at once on this page. Less able children should focus on one aspect of speech punctuation at a time, and should be supported by templates such as the one on page 48, 'Model dialogue'.

Back at school
The children apply the skill to the context of story writing.

p104 GRACE DARLING

Objective
Join sentences through using a widening range of conjunctions. (Y3, T3, S5)

Lesson context
Use this homework at the redrafting stage of writing as a way of helping children to focus on improving their sentence construction.

Setting the homework
Define the term *conjunction,* using the definition and examples on the sheet.

Differentiation
All children should be able to do the cloze exercise with more or less support, but some children may struggle with the terminology at this stage.

Back at school
Quickly go over the exercise, then ask the children to look at the first draft of a piece of their own writing. See if they can improve any of their sentences by joining two short sentences into one with a conjunction or by substituting a different conjunction where they have used 'and'.

p105 TIME SEQUENCE

Objective
Investigate how words and phrases can signal time sequences. (Y3, T3, S6)

Lesson context
This homework is good preparation for writing or redrafting writing in the narrative or recount genre as it helps children learn different ways of linking events thus helping to avoid the 'and then' syndrome.

Setting the homework
Explain that the task is based on the Battle of Hastings. The task is to choose appropriate time-sequence words and phrases to fill the gaps. All the words and phrases in the list should be used only once.

Differentiation
The more able should be particularly encouraged to find additional time-sequence words.

Back at school
Go over the exercise and share new time-sequence words that the children have found. The children should apply the skill by looking over old stories and recounts that they have written.

THE ANT AND THE GRASSHOPPER

Objective
Retell main points of a story in sequence. (Y3, T3, T1)

Lesson context
This homework is a good follow-up to work on story sequence or the organisation of stories into paragraphs. This sheet also goes well with page 105, 'Time sequence', as children will use words that signal time sequences as clues for re-sequencing the fable.

Setting the homework
Tell the children to read the text carefully *before* cutting it up.

Differentiation
The fable on the sheet has a simple 'linear' plot. More able children could be given a more complex story to sequence and retell, eg one with a subplot or a flashback.

Back at school
Ask for volunteers to retell the fable. Ask the other children to listen carefully. Did they get everything in the right order? Did they miss anything out? Discuss how the text was re-sequenced. What clues revealed the first and last paragraphs and those inbetween?

WILL-O'-THE-WYKES AND BOGLES

Objective
Refer to significant aspects of the text, eg opening, build-up, atmosphere, and to know how language is used to create these. (Y3, T3, T2)

Lesson context
This homework is a good preparation for a shared reading study of how an author uses language to create atmosphere, or writing a story with a focus on building atmosphere through language.

Setting the homework
Explain that part of our enjoyment of a story is in the build-up and atmosphere as much as in the events themselves.

Differentiation
Less able children should focus on more basic points of literature study such as plot and character.

Back at school
Talk about definitions of the atmosphere created – anything in the 'spooky' or 'frightening' line will do. Discuss which words and phrases were highlighted. Debate what might happen next. Ask the children to write the next scene.

p108 FIRST OR THIRD?

Objective
Distinguish between first and third person accounts. (Y3, T3, T3)

Lesson context
This homework is a good preparation for story-writing as it can help the children to make a conscious choice between the use of the first or third person.

Setting the homework
Remind the children that a story may be written in the first person, from the narrator's or main character's point of view, or the third person, where the narrator, is not a character in the story.

Differentiation
Children who have not grasped the concept of person should work on that (see pages 35 and 78).

Back at school
Share examples of children's own passages. Discuss the question at the bottom of the page. Generally, the advantage of first person is that it is the best way of getting into a character's thoughts and feelings. The advantage of third person is that the author has an 'objective' point of view and can see and know everything.

p109 STRANGER THAN FICTION?

Objective
Select some real-life adventures and compare them with fiction. (Y3, T3, T4)

Lesson context
This homework is a good preparation for writing fiction and is particularly helpful at the planning stage as it explores the complex relationship between real life and fiction.

Setting the homework
Explain to the children that the purpose of the homework is to study a real-life pirate to see how he compares with fictional pirates. In order to get the most out of this, children will need to be familiar with fictional pirates. Page 110, 'Pirates', can be used to help with this.

Differentiation
You may wish to ask less able children to omit the highlighting of adjectives exercise.

Back at school
Discuss how Blackbeard compares with the fictional pirates that the children know. In some ways he is 'stranger than fiction'. His appearance is as theatrical as any fictional pirate, as is his death with his skull being used as a drinking cup. It is interesting to note that Blackbeard is the model for many fictional pirates.

p110 PIRATES

Objective
Discuss characters' feelings, behaviour and relationships. (Y3, T3, T5)

Lesson context
This homework can be used alongside page 109, 'Stranger than fiction?', to compare real and fictional pirates, or as the starting point for exploring character in fiction. If you are using it for the latter, the children will need to be familiar with the whole in book or film form.

Setting the homework
Explain that both texts give us clues about the characters' feelings and relationships. Children should first study the basic character description, then look for evidence for the characters' feelings and relationships.

Differentiation
You may wish to ask less able children to omit the highlighting of adjectives exercise.

Back at school
Discuss the two characters. Long John's appearance is rough and forbidding, but at this point in the story he appears to be a kindly, cheerful person. Captain Hook comes across as a cruel man who dominates others by fear.

p111 SANDWICH FILLINGS

Objective
Compare forms or types of humour. (Y3, T3, T6)

Lesson context
Humour is an effective way to explore wordplay and patterns in poetry. Thus, this homework is a good follow-up to a lesson on poetry writing.

Setting the homework
Talk about different kinds of humour. Ask the children to read the poem and talk about why it is funny. They should all try to write a similar poem, and then if they feel able, try to write a different kind of poem or joke and compare it with the poem on this sheet.

Back at school
Share the poems the children have written. Discuss the different kinds of humorous poems they know and say why they are funny, building up a class list of the ways authors and poets create humour.

p112 ELEANOR RIGBY

Objective
Select, prepare, read aloud and recite by heart poetry. (Y3, T3, T7)

Lesson context
Use as one of a series of lessons on poetry. This homework would go particularly well with a study of songs, ballads and oral poetry. Note that it can be used as a pair with 'I'm Only Sleeping' – another Lennon/McCartney song – in *100 Literacy Hours: Year 3* (page 146).

Setting the homework
Ideally, play a recording of 'Eleanor Rigby' a number of times to familiarise the children with the tune. This will help them to learn the words by heart later on.

Back at school
Ask for volunteers to recite or sing the words from memory. The song is a good stimulus for further work on the theme of loneliness.

p113 COMPARING POEMS

Objective
Compare and contrast works by the same author. (Y3, T3, T8)

Lesson context
Use as part of a series of lessons on poetry to compare poems by the same writer. Note that the comparison sheet works best if the two works have some significant differences.

Setting the homework
Choose two poems, songs or ballads by the same writer (or writers) to compare. You could use page 112 and a contrasting Lennon/McCartney song, eg 'I'm Only Sleeping' on page 146 of *100 Literacy Hours: Year 3*.

Differentiation
Less able children may have difficulty writing about verse form. They could be given a simpler version of the sheet with this section omitted. You could ask more able children to go into more detail when writing their short essay.

Back at school
Share the children's ideas about the two songs or poems.

p114 ROBIN HOOD

Objective
Plot a sequence of episodes modelled on a known story. (Y3, T3, T10)

Lesson context
This homework can be used as the first step in developing children's writing from short stories to longer stories in chapters. The material is also a valuable follow-up to work on Robin Hood in *100 Literacy Hours: Year 3* (pages 175-83).

Setting the homework
It is recommended that a version of the Robin Hood legend in either prose or ballad form is studied before setting this homework (note that the unit in *100 Literacy Hours: Year 3* is based on *Robin Hood and the Sheriff* by Julian Atterton, Walker Books). Explain to the children that modern authors and film-makers often use the characters and settings as the basis for new adventures, eg as in the film *Robin Hood, Prince of Thieves*. Therefore, the children should not be afraid to make up completely new adventures for Robin and his men. The idea is to combine these with retellings of some of the traditional adventures, and a whole new version of the Robin Hood story is the result.

Differentiation
Less able children should concentrate first on retelling the episodes listed.

Back at school
The best retellings and new adventures can be collected and edited into a class book about Robin Hood.

p115 SLEEPING BEAUTY

Objective
Write a character's own account of an incident in a story. (Y3, T3, T12)

Lesson context
Writing a character's account of a story event is a very good way to explore characters in a text. This homework is intended as a preparatory exercise. The skill can then be applied to a shared text that the class is studying in detail. The exercise also links well with work on first, second and third person (see page 78, 'Let's get personal').

Setting the homework
Revise work on person (see page 78), then recap on the story of 'Sleeping Beauty'. A good way to do this is to brainstorm the opening scenes of the story, leaving the rest to be told by the extract of the sheet. Ask the children to write about the extract, in the first person, from the viewpoint of one of the characters. Note that they can choose any of the characters – an interesting and amusing version of the story could be told by the kitchen maid, for example. However, if the children choose a character other than the prince they may wish to choose another episode from the story.

Differentiation
Less able children could use the sample as a 'starter'. This will get them going using the first person and an appropriate point of view. More able children should be encouraged to explore their character's thoughts, feelings, doubts and motives in more depth.

Back at school
Share what has been written. Then, either continue the exercise until the whole story is complete or apply the skill to another shared text.

p116 IMPROVE A STORY

Objective
Write more extended stories. (Y3, T3, T13)

Lesson context
Use this homework to help the children write extended stories. There are two main ways of doing this, both equally important. One is to develop a series of adventures that can be developed into paragraphs (see page 114, 'Robin Hood'). The other is to develop the detail in which the story is told. This is the main focus of this sheet, though it also includes writing additional adventures.

Setting the homework
Explain how stories can be improved by including more detail. For example, the short description of Pegleg could be compared with the description of Blackbeard on page 109 or Captain Hook on page 110. Ask the children to plan some more adventures for Pegleg.

Differentiation
This homework focuses on making a good story better. However, some children may not yet have reached the stage where they can write a simple, straightforward story. Such children would be better writing a simple pirate adventure based on a map (see page 188 of *100 Literacy Hours: Year 3*).

Back at school
Compare ways of improving the story. Share ideas for additional adventures. The children could then either write the full-length story of Pegleg the pirate in chapters, or apply the skill to another topic.

p117 BOOK REVIEW (2)

Objective
Write book reviews for a specified audience, based on evaluations of plot, characters and language. (Y3, T3, T14)

Lesson context
This homework is a good follow-up to individual reading. Whereas work on a shared text should lead to detailed study of character, plot and language, a book review, which touches on these aspects more briefly, is more suitable for a book that a child has read alone.

Setting the homework
This sheet can be given out on an individual basis when children finish their individual reading books. Early in the term, it is worth going over the writing frame on the sheet with all the children. Explain that the phrases and the paragraph layout act as a 'skeleton' for a book review.

Differentiation
A simpler book review sheet may be found in *100 Literacy Hours: Year 3*, page 183. This gives boxes and headings, but is not intended as a framework for an essay in paragraphs. More able children should be encouraged to write in more depth and detail.

Back at school
It is a good idea to have a class folder for book reviews. When children have written a book review, and you have read it, it can be placed in the folder for other children to read.

p118 MOTHS AND MOONSHINE

Objective
Write poetry that uses alliteration to create effects. (Y3, T3, T15)

Lesson context
Use as part of a series of lessons on poetry. Note that work on alliteration goes particularly well with work on alphabets and acrostics.

Setting the homework
Define *alliteration*. Note that it is sounds which *alliterate,* not *letters,* so *f* and *ph* alliterate, hard *c* and *k,* and so on. When the children write their poems, ask them to focus on alliteration only – they do not have to make them rhyme as well.

Differentiation
Less able children should be spared the more complex points of the definition (see above) and should use the simpler definition given on the homework sheet. Explain that a few lines of poetry or an alliterative slogan will be sufficient for the writing task.

Back at school
Share the children's alliterative poems. Investigate alliteration further by exploring its use in advertising and in early English poetry – eg in a good translation of Anglo-Saxon riddles.

p119 BANK LETTER

Objective
Read examples of letters written for a range of purposes. (Y3, T3, T16)

Lesson context
Study of the conventions of formal and informal letter writing. Note that this homework is not suitable for a first attempt at setting out a formal letter; it is best used for further practice of this skill.

Setting the homework
Quickly revise the conventions of formal letter writing. Ask the children to use the ideas in Tom's informal letter to Jim as the basis for a formal letter of complaint to the bank.

Differentiation
Children who struggle to write informal letters with correct conventions of layout and paragraphing should not be given this sheet, but should be asked to write and address a letter to a friend instead.

Back at school
Examine the children's use of formal letter conventions, and the style and language used in their responses.

p120 SEASIDE INDEX

Objective
Scan indexes to locate information quickly and accurately. (Y3, T3, T17)

Lesson context
Use this homework as a preparation for real research using contents, indexes and so on.

Setting the homework
Explain to the children that they should use the homework sheet as a starting point, and then move on to a real reference book if a suitable one is available.

Differentiation
It might be a good idea to leave out the timing element for some children so that they do not feel under pressure.

Back at school
Apply the skill to a real research context.

p121 BE A LIBRARIAN

Objective
Locate books by classification. (Y3, T3, T18)

Lesson context
This homework is a valuable preliminary to using the library for research. It can also be linked to page 56, 'Fiction and non-fiction', as this homework takes the skill of sorting fiction and non-fiction a step further.

Setting the homework
Briefly recap on the main points of the Dewey Decimal system (eg by using page 197 from *100 Literacy Hours: Year 3*). Then ask the children to imagine that they are librarians and a new batch of non-fiction books has just come in. The librarian's job is to classify them and put them on the shelves. Knowing the range of numbers is a great help in using a library.

Differentiation
The hard part for the less able is linking titles to categories, especially when the links are not obvious. Parents can be asked specifically to help with this.

Back at school
Visit the school library and investigate the Dewey Decimal system in use with real books. Apply the skills to a research task.

p122 LETTER TO AN AUTHOR

Objective
Write letters to authors about books. (Y3, T3, T20)

Lesson context
This homework is a good follow-up to completing the study of a shared text or a preliminary to an author's visit. It also helps to reinforce skills of letter writing.

Setting the homework
Explain that the writing frame is only a guide. Encourage the children to write what they really want to say. The writing frame gives good ways of starting and ending a letter, but the children could use their own thoughts for the middle.

Differentiation
Less able children should follow the writing frame closely.

Back at school
Discuss the drafts of the letters, redraft them to make them as good as possible. Rather than bombarding an author or their publisher with letters, the class could pool their ideas in a whole-class letter to one chosen author and send that.

p123 JOHN KEATS

Objective
Use ICT to bring to a published form – discuss relevance of layout, font, and so on – to the audience. (Y3, T3, T21)

Lesson context
This homework should be used in preparation for the publication of the children's writing through ICT. It will provide them with practice in planning layout and presentation.

Setting the homework
Emphasise that the homework does not depend on children having a computer at home. It is preparation for doing a similar activity at school. However, if children do have the technology at home, they should be encouraged to use it. The guidance at the top of the sheet should be modified to take into account the ICT skills that have been taught. Explain to children that, when sketching their layout, they can use lines to represent the text. If possible, provide the children with A4 graph paper for sketching the plan.

Differentiation
This will depend on children's own computer skills and knowledge. Most children should be able to sketch a plan. Realising it on a computer will be the difficult part.

Back at school
Discuss different layout ideas, highlighting the pros and cons of the various concepts. If possible, get the children to translate their plans – modified as necessary – onto the computer. To save time, it would be worth making the text available electronically, so that the children can concentrate on presentation, rather than on entering the text.

p124 GUY FAWKES

Objective
Experiment with recounting the same event in a variety of ways. (Y3, T3, T22)

Lesson context
This homework could therefore be used to prepare for a lesson on exploring texts or as a preparation for creative writing.

Setting the homework
Explain to the children that the lives of famous people are often told and retold in many ways. For this reason they should have the confidence to develop the information about Guy Fawkes in any way they wish. The series of letters, for example, changes the biographical recount into an autobiographical account.

Differentiation
More able children should be encouraged to develop their own format for retelling the story.

Back at school
Share the children's letters by Guy Fawkes and their ideas for other formats. Work on Guy Fawkes could be further developed, or the same approach applied to a different or more substantial piece of text. The children could write up some of their ideas for retelling the story.

p125 LETTERS

Objective
Organise letters into simple paragraphs. (Y3, T3, T23)

Lesson context
This homework provides reinforcement of the first steps of paragraphing non-fiction.

Setting the homework
Before giving out the sheets, revise the points given in the guidelines at the top of the page. If some children have access to a computer at home, they could be encouraged to word-process their letter.

Differentiation
Note that this homework focuses on the first steps of paragraphing; it is therefore not suitable more able children. They could be asked to write a formal letter (eg complaining about an issue) in block paragraphs. Less able children might be helped by being given the clue that the letter will divide neatly into three paragraphs.

Back at school
Check the homework, particularly how well the children have applied the skill to their own personal letter where appropriate. Where necessary, provide reinforcement of the skill.

p126 BOOK ORGANISATION

Objective
Make alphabetically ordered texts. (Y3, T3, T24)

Lesson context
This homework is a good follow-up to work on alphabetical order, and index and referencing systems.

Setting the homework
Revise the book-language terms *contents, index* and *glossary*. Discuss different ways of organising non-fiction books. Sometimes the subject itself will suggest an arrangement. Historical topics, for example, will often be in chronological order. However, organisation is often alphabetical. This homework allows children to experiment with different ways of organising information.

Differentiation
Less able children could complete the first task only. More able could be asked to think of some of the difficult words that might appear in a book on the solar system and write a short glossary.

Back at school
The skills developed by this homework can be used in planning an extended work of non-fiction, perhaps on a group or class basis.

p127 CRABS

Objective
Summarise in writing the content of a passage or text. (Y3, T3, T26)

Lesson context
This summary exercise is the next step from page 60, 'Hurricane', as the children have to pick out five main points and then rewrite them in a paragraph. Summary exercises are a valuable preparation for cross-curricular research, as they give children the skill of processing information from reference texts without merely copying.

Setting the homework
Explain that there are about ten facts in this passage and it is impossible to include them all in a summary (or it would not be a summary!). Children should therefore pick out the five facts that they think are the most important or interesting. Tell them to check that their five facts are spread through the whole passage (they should not take just the first five). The next step is to *rewrite* them in a paragraph. Stress that this is more than just writing their facts one after another. The paragraph should be written in sentences. Sometimes it will sound better if two facts are placed in one sentence and linked by 'and' or another conjunction (see page 104, 'Grace Darling'). Explain that the word 'crab(s)' should not be used in every sentence. Using pronouns instead in some sentences will help the paragraph to sound like a connected whole.

Differentiation
Children who found page 60 difficult could be asked to omit the third task.

Back at school
Share the summaries and discuss how well they meet the criteria explained above.

W Name:

Adding -ing

Spelling -**ing** words can be tricky. Try to remember these rules:

Many words add -**ing** without any change of spelling:

shout → shout**ing** laugh → laugh**ing**

Words ending in **e**, drop the **e** before adding -**ing**:

giggle → giggl**ing** race → rac**ing**

Words with a short vowel before the last consonant, double the final consonant:

swim → swimm**ing** win → winn**ing**

- Add -**ing** to the verbs below. The first one has been done for you.

Word	Word +ing
clap	clapping
go	
hope	
jump	
like	
look	
pull	
ride	
rub	
say	
shop	
smile	
take	
try	
walk	
write	

Dear Helper,

Objective: to understand how spellings of verbs may alter when *-ing* is added.

Remind your child that a *verb* is an action word. Check that your child understands which rule applies to each word and has written the *-ing* word correctly.

Name:

A little snivel

- Add -**el** or -**le** to each of the word beginnings below.

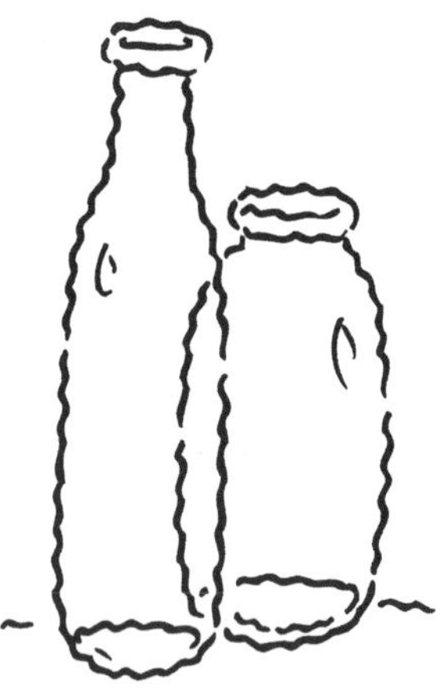

WORD BEGINNING	ADD el OR le	WORD BEGINNING	ADD el OR le
ab		lab	
barr		midd	
bott		mod	
cab		mudd	
cam		parc	
cand		possib	
circ		pudd	
cru		quarr	
doub		simp	
examp		squirr	
fu		tab	
gigg		terrib	
gosp		tow	
horrib		trav	
hot		tunn	
icic		unc	
jew		vow	
kenn		wobb	

Dear Helper,

Objective: to learn and use the spelling pattern -*le*.

Encourage your child to say the word (by adding an 'l' sound at the word beginning) and then to choose one of the endings to write in the adjacent column.

W Name:

Prefix game

Prefixes

un	de	dis	re
un	de	dis	re
un	de	dis	re
un	de	dis	re
un	de	dis	re

Roots

well	frost	please	build
happy	code	agree	fill
tidy	form	honest	visit
lucky	fuse	appear	play
do	mist	obey	write

How to play

1 Cut out and shuffle the cards.
2 Deal the cards to each player. The players should separate their cards into roots and prefixes.
3 Player 1 puts down any card – a prefix or a root.
4 Player 2 must then try to finish the word by using a prefix or a root from their cards. They win a point for making a word, and an extra point for defining it!
5 Player 2 then puts down a new card and it is the next player's turn to finish the word.
6 If a player cannot finish the word, the next player can try to do so.
7 The winner is the player with the most points once all the cards have been put down.

PHOTOCOPIABLE

Dear Helper,

Objective: to recognise and spell common prefixes and how these affect meanings.

Play this game with your child. It may help to colour the root and prefix cards different colours. Remind your child that a *prefix* is a word-part added to the beginning of a word to change its meaning. For each word made ask: 'How has adding the prefix changed the meaning of the word?'

Name:

Multi-purpose prefixes

These prefixes are often used to make up new words:

Prefix	Meaning
anti	against
cyber	to do with the Internet
Euro	to do with Europe
hyper	very big
mega	very big
micro	very small
mini	small
multi	many
super	very good or large
web	to do with the Internet

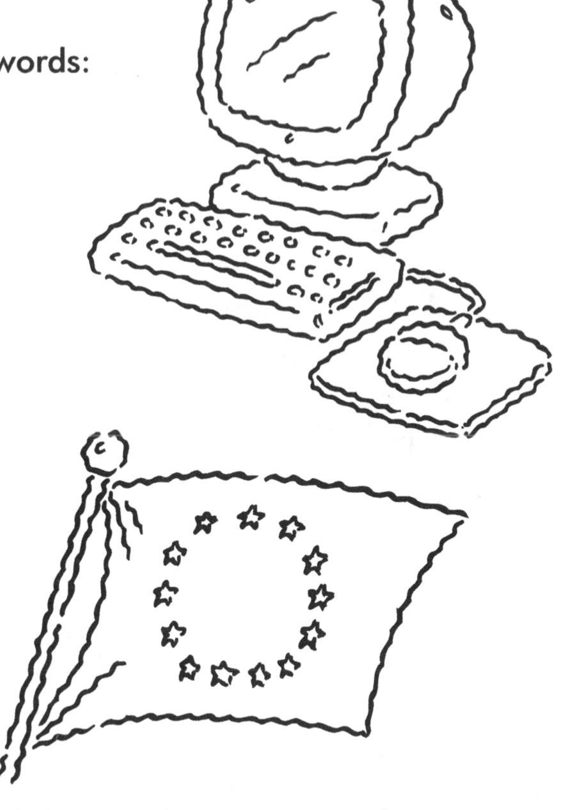

- Look at these examples of new words, and then make up some of your own.

Prefix	Meaning
megaproblem	very big problem
minihomework	a small homework
webschool	a school on the Internet

Dear Helper,

Objective: to make up new words using prefixes.

Remind your child that a *prefix* is a word-part added to the beginning of a word to change its meaning. Go over the prefixes and their meanings, then help your child to brainstorm new words using the prefixes.

Name:

Nice day out

- Rewrite the story below without using the words **big**, **little**, **like**, **good**, **nice** or **nasty**. Choose suitable **synonyms** (words of similar meaning) from those given. Or use other ones that you think are better!

big	**little**	**like**	**good**	**nice**	**nasty**
bulky	miniature	admire	delicious	delightful	atrocious
burly	minute	adore	excellent	enjoyable	dirty
enormous	puny	be fond of	fantastic	friendly	disgusting
gigantic	short	enjoy	ideal	fine	filthy
huge	small	fancy	pleasant	kind	foul
large	tiny	love	valuable	perfect	gross
massive	wee	prefer	worthy	wonderful	unpleasant

Savi was looking forward to a nice day out with Time Travel Tours.

"Which time would you like to visit?" asked the guide.

"136 million BC, please," said Savi.

After a good journey in the time machine, Savi stepped out int the Jurassic jungle. He was surprised how big the trees were. "I think I'll go for a little stroll," he said.

Savi had not gone far when he saw a creature like a big crocodile walking on its hind legs. Savi felt so little and helpless. He turned and ran back to the time machine, which took off quickly.

"What was that nasty creature?" gasped Savi.

"An Allosaurus, I think," said the guide.

"Yuk!" said Savi. "Can you take me somewhere nice instead?"

Dear Helper,

Objective: to use synonyms of 'big', 'little', 'like', 'good', 'nice' and 'nasty'.

Discuss the synonyms for each word with your child. Together, see if you can think of others or find others in a thesaurus. Help your child to choose the most appropriate synonyms to fit the story.

Name:

W

Mash

asked	cried	declared	exclaimed	explained
pleaded	replied	said	shouted	snapped

- Choose from the synonyms of **said** above to fill the gaps in the story. You do not have to use all the words, and you can use any word more than once.

Schoolbot is a robot who has taken the place of one of the children at St Mark's Primary School.

At last the bell rang for lunch.

"Hey, Schoolbot!" ________________ Tom. "Come and sit at our lunch table!"

"I am very sorry," ________________ Schoolbot, "but I do not eat."

"Not eat!" ________________ Tom.

"No," ________________ Schoolbot. "I recharge my battery instead."

"Will you come and sit with us anyway?" ________________ Tom.

Schoolbot went with Tom into the dining room and they sat down. Unfortunately, St Mark's Primary School has some very strict dinner ladies.

"Now, what's this?" ________________ Mrs MacDuff to Schoolbot. "Why are you not eating?"

"Because it would give me a short circuit," ________________ Schoolbot.

"No excuses!" ________________ Mrs MacDuff, and spooned mashed potato into Schoolbot's mouth. There was a bang and a flash and Schoolbot fell to the floor.

Dear Helper,

Objective: to choose alternative words to 'said' to make dialogue more interesting.

Remind your child that a *synonym* is a word of similar meaning to another. Read this passage with your child and experiment with different synonyms of 'said' in the gaps. Then let your child make the final decision about which synonyms to write in.

Name:

Karen's secret

- Highlight all the punctuation in the pasage below and then read the story aloud. Make your reading as realistic as possible.

Schoolbot is a story about a boy called David, who sends a robot to school in his place. In this section, Karen tells Kavita that she has fallen in love with Schoolbot.

Karen whispered her secret to Kavita.

"But you can't be!" exclaimed Kavita.

"Why not?" said Karen.

"Because he's a robot! You can't love bits of metal and wire!"

Kavita thought about this for a moment. "Why not? My dad loves his car."

Kavita sighed. "But it's not the same. I mean, how could you kiss Schoolbot? It would be like kissing a washing machine!"

"At least his breath won't smell!"

Kavita decided to try something else. "Why don't you have a date with David, instead?"

Karen laughed. "David's horrible! All he does is sit at home all day and watch TV."

"At least he's human."

"Well if he's human, I prefer a robot!" Karen tried her best to explain how she felt. "I love Schoolbot because he is good at lessons and sports, because he's polite and because his little tin nose is so cute."

"But he's got no emotions – he can never love you back!"

Tears began to roll down Karen's cheeks. "Oh, Kavita, I know! What should I do?"

Dear Helper,

Objective: to take account of sentences, speech marks, exclamation marks and commas when reading aloud.

Go over the punctuation with your child so that they can use it as a support for an effective reading. Read the story aloud with your child, if necessary.

Name:

S

Verb tables

A **verb** is a 'doing' or 'action' word.
Verb tables like the one below show different forms of verbs:

singular (one)

plural (more than one)

person: **first** (I, we); **second** (you); **third** (he, she, it, they)

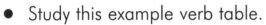

- Study this example verb table.

To work:

Simple present tense	**Singular**	**Plural**
First person	I work	we work
Second person	you work	you work
Third person	he/she/it works	they work

- Complete the following verb tables:

To play:

Simple present tense	**Singular**	**Plural**
First person		
Second person		
Third person		

To sing:

Simple present tense	**Singular**	**Plural**
First person		
Second person		
Third person		

Dear Helper,

Objective: to use verb tenses accurately.

Help your child to understand the information presented in the verb table before helping them to complete the two blank tables correctly.

Name:

Hot Sleepysaurus

- Highlight all the speech marks in this story and then read it aloud.

The Sleepysaurus is a creature like a rock garden that turns up at Bell Street Flats. This is what happened when it began to get too hot:

The Sleepysaurus lay there in the sun getting hotter and hotter, and we all thought a lot.

"We can't carry baths," said Niki.

"And the Mean Man has taken away the hose pipe," said Rashid.

"What about buckets?" I said.

We got our buckets, and then we looked at the Sleepysaurus.

"How many bucketfuls do we need?" I asked Rashid and Niki.

"Hundreds!" said Rashid.

"Thousands!" said Niki.

"Millions!" I said.

"Billions!" said Rashid.

"Trillions!" said Niki.

"Hundreds of thousands of millions of billions of trillions!" I said. "And there's only one tap in the yard!"

from *Our Sleepysaurus* © 1988 Martin Waddell

Dear Helper,

Objective: to identify speech marks in reading.

When your child has highlighted all the speech marks, take it in turns to read the dialogue and the narrated text (ie the text not in speech marks).

Name:

S

Capital letters in speech

When you are writing speech, always use a capital letter after the first speech marks:

"**S**top!" said Miss Marvel.

When a line of speech is divided into two parts, the second part begins with a capital letter *only* if the first part ends with a full stop:

"Stop!" said Miss Marvel. "**T**hat's all wrong!"

But:

"Wait," said Miss Marvel, "**u**ntil all the children are here."

- Add capital letters to the dialogue below. Don't forget the names and places!

"tomorrow we are going on a school trip to london," Miss Marvel announced.

"miss marvel, if I get travel sick," asked Karen, "what shall I do?"

"don't worry, karen, we'll take a bucket," said miss marvel.

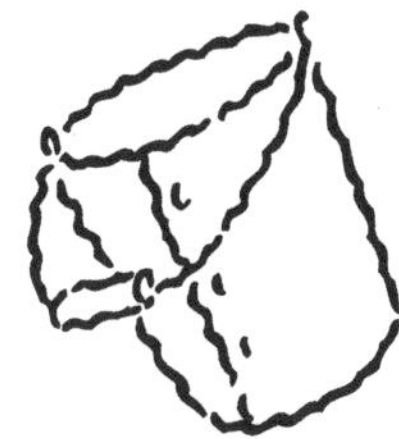

"i get sick as well," said fifteen other children.

"oh dear!" said the teacher. "that's rather a lot of you!"

"never mind," said tom, "we'll take a bathtub instead!"

Dear Helper,

Objective: to use capital letters to mark the start of direct speech.

Discuss with your child the use of capital letters to begin names, places and sentences. Then go over the explanation of this additional use of capital letters.

PHOTOCOPIABLE

Name:

Shopping game

potatoes	trainers	TV	guitar
pizza	socks	VCR	pipe organ
bread	computer	DVD player	paintbrush
pasta	printer	cassettes	hammer
jeans	keyboard	clarinet	pliers
T-shirt	mouse	cello	screwdriver

- What did you buy when you went shopping? To find out, cut out the cards, shuffle them, turn them face down and then pick out up to five cards.
- Write the items in a list like this:

I bought a paintbrush, jeans, T-shirt **and** a mouse.

____

____

Remember!
Use a comma after each item, but not before **and**.

Dear Helper,

Objective: to use commas to separate items in a list.

Play this game with your child. Take it in turn to select cards and write lists. Add to the variety by making more object cards – cutting up an old catalogue is a good way to do this. Have fun by trying to explain what you plan to do with the items.

Name:

T

Story settings

- Read these story settings. Underline or highlight the words and phrases that describe each scene.

That summer, we went to Jamaica. The first thing I noticed when I stepped off the plane was the heat – a clinging, steamy heat like a Turkish bath. Then there was the tangled tropical jungle. It was like going back into the Jurassic age. By the time we reached our hotel it was dusk, and the air was full of the music of cicadas and tree frogs.

The street was a very ordinary street, a street of rows. There were rows of houses in dull red brick - all the same. There were rows of cars, one on each side of the straight stretch of tarmac. A row of shops at the top end offered some variety. The biggest shop, the Supersave supermarket, had huge glass windows with posters shouting about the latest bargains. There had once been a bank next to it, but that was now boarded up and the boards were covered with grafitti.

My name is Sarah and I am the first human being to see this scene with my own eyes: Mount Olympus on Mars. It is a volcano, but is much bigger than any mountain on Earth. As I gaze up to its jagged, red peak, I feel that I could climb up it all the way back to Earth. Let me tell you how I got to be in this awesome place.

The tunnel was low, and it was very hot. Tanis crept along on all fours with great care. He was afraid that he would spring one of the traps left by the dead Pharoah to protect his tomb. Suddenly he came to a great chamber. He stood up, raised his lamp, and was amazed at the brilliantly coloured pictures on the walls.

Dear Helper,

Objective: to compare a range of story settings and select words and phrases that describe scenes.
Read these story settings with your child and discuss what brings them to life.

Name:

Picture the setting

- Choose one of these picture settings and write a detailed description of it. Use your imagination to add to what you can see.

Outer space

Enchanted castle

Deserted house

School

Dear Helper,

Objective: to write a description of a story setting using a picture stimulus.

Talk about each of the pictures with your child and help them to pick the one they find most interesting.

Name:

Presenting dialogue (1)

When dialogue is presented in a story, a new line is started for every change of speaker. This makes it much clearer for the reader to follow.

- Read this example and highlight the first word of every change of speaker.

"Oh Sam! You've made a puddle on the kitchen floor!" groaned Lucy.

"Woof, woof," replied Sam.

"Yes, I know that you're proud of it," said Lucy, "but you should have done it outside!"

"Woof, woof," replied Sam.

"Yes, I know the door was shut, but why didn't you ask me to open it? All you have to say is..."

"Woof, woof," barked Sam.

"Yes, that's it!" said Lucy.

- Now try it yourself by completing this conversation:

"Lucy! Has that puppy chewed my cushions?" said Mum.

"Sorry, Mum, but she's only a puppy!" said Lucy.

Dear Helper,

Objective: to understand how dialogue is presented in stories.

Spend some time helping your child to analyse the example of dialogue. Make sure that they notice exclamation marks, questions marks, commas and capital letters, as well as the main teaching point – that each new speaker starts a new line.

Name:

Presenting dialogue (2)

When dialogue is presented in a story, a new indented line is started for every change of speaker. Note that only the first line of a speech is indented. The following lines begin at the margin.

- Read this example and highlight the first word of every change of speaker.

"Listen, Sam, that must be the newspaper boy bringing today's paper!" said Lucy.

"Woof, woof," replied Sam.

"I wonder if you can remember what you learned at dog school," said Lucy. "When I give the word, take the paper to Dad. Now fetch!"

"Woof, woof," replied Sam as he bounded to the door. There was a sound of crumpling newspaper and then Sam bounded into the lounge where Dad was sitting.

"Did it work?" shouted Lucy.

"Sort of," said Dad. "He fetched the paper, but it's all torn."

"Woof, woof," barked Sam.

- Now try it yourself by completing this conversation:

"Walkies!" shouted Lucy.

"Woof, woof!" replied Sam as he went to get his lead.

Dear Helper,

Objective: to understand how dialogue is presented in stories.

Spend some time helping your child to analyse the example of dialogue, particularly the main teaching point, that there is a new *indented* line for every change of speaker.

Name:

T

Schoolbot

- Read this play scene and think about how you would prepare it for performance.

Scene 1: A classroom in the year 2010. The children are coming into the classroom, among them is a robot called Schoolbot.

Teacher: Good morning, children. (To Schoolbot) Who are you?

Schoolbot: (*in a metallic voice*) My name is Schoolbot.

Teacher: (*looking around*) Where is David?

Schoolbot: David sent me in his place.

Teacher: Why did he do that?

Schoolbot: Because he says that school is boring.

Teacher: We aren't in the entertainment business, you know.

Schoolbot: (*looking around*) So I see.

Teacher: If David doesn't come to school, he won't learn anything and he won't be able to get a job.

Schoolbot: I will get a job for him.

Teacher: I'll have to see the headmistress about this later. (*To the class*) Get out your maths books and do numbers 1-100 starting on page 32. (*Aside*) That should keep them quiet for an hour.

A few moments later.

Schoolbot: I have finished.

Teacher: What? Already?

Schoolbot: My Pentium 1000 brain can perform a million calculations per second.

Teacher: (*sighing*) Now there's quick mental maths for you!

Extension

- On a separate piece of paper, write extra scenes for the play. Think about, for example, what Schoolbot is like at other subjects such as PE and ICT. What happens at lunchtime? What might happen when David gets bored at home?

Dear Helper,

Objective: to read, prepare and present playscripts.
Read the script with your child and help them to prepare it for performance. Discuss ideas for extra scenes.

PHOTOCOPIABLE

T

Name:

Whale poems

- Read aloud and compare these poems.

from **The Ballad of the Whale**

"Thar she blows!" the lookout cries,
As he sees the fountain spout.
"Lower the boats!" the captain cries
And the whale boats are swung out.

"Heave her close!" the harpoonist cries,
As he flings his sharp harpoon.
"She sounds, she sounds!" the oarsmen cry,
"But we will have her soon!"

"Stow the barrels!" the captain cries
"The barrels full of oil."
"'Tis liquid gold!" the whalers cry,
"Reward for all our toil!"

Anon

thar = there   sounds = dives

Whale

In this room, and the next, and the next,
you will see a whale; huge creatures once found
in all oceans of the world,
criss-crossing the waters,
sending the signals we failed to hear.
Till whales all but disappeared,
and then it was far too late.

We chased this one for several days,
repaired the damage the harpoon made,
and now this whale is as good as new.
This was the one they called 'Big Blue'.

Brian Moses

Dear Helper,

Objective: to read aloud poems comparing different views of the same subject.
Share the reading of these poems with your child. Discuss the different attitudes to the whale expressed in each one.

Name:

T

Comparing poems

- Compare two poems on the same subject by filling in this table.

	Title:	Title:
	Poet:	Poet:
Subject: (Explain in your own words what the poem says.)		
Verse form: (Is it written in rhyming or non-rhyming verse? If it is in rhyming verse, what is the pattern of rhymes?)		
Interesting words and phrases (Jot down any interesting words or phrases and say why you chose them.)		
Opinion: (Which of the two poems do you like best? Why?)		

Dear Helper,

Objective: to compare two poems on the same subject.

Your child will have been given two poems to compare. Read them together. Help your child to fill in the table by discussing both poems and helping your child to pick out illustrative words and phrases.

Name:

I had a boat

- One of these of poems is a **rhyming** poem and the other is a **non-rhyming** poem. Say which is which, then examine the way they are set out.

I had a boat, and the boat had wings;
    And I dreamed that we went flying
Over the heads of queens and kings,
    Over the souls of dead and dying,
Up among the stars and the great white rings,
    And where the Moon on her back is lying.

Mary Coleridge

My boat is my escape.
I push it out
onto the lake
and lie back
and look at the sky
and I feel I am
    floating up there
      far away
        from my
          problems.

Amy Reeves

Dear Helper,

Objective: to distinguish between rhyming and non-rhyming poetry and comment on layout.

Your child will need most help with examining the way the poems are set out. Help them to look carefully at line indentations, punctuation, use of capital letters and so on. They should also read each poem aloud and think about the effect the line breaks have on the way the poem is read.

Name:

T

Book review (1)

- Use this framework to help you write about a story you have read.

Paragraph 1
Give the title and author and briefly explain what the story is about.

Paragraph 2
Describe the main character in the book. Quote some words and phrases that describe the character. Say what you liked and disliked about the character.

Paragraph 3
Describe the main place in the book. Quote some words and phrases that describe the place.

Paragraph 4
Say what you liked best about the book, for example, describe an exciting scene and say why you liked it.

Dear Helper,

Objective: to express views about a story, identifying specific words and phrases.
Your child should be able to remember the plot and characters, but may need help in finding suitable words and phrases to quote.

T Name:

Model dialogue

- Look at this example of dialogue and notice the use of punctuation and indentations.

Tim and Tom spent most of the afternoon in the shed trying to make aeroplanes from kits – but everything seemed to go wrong.

"Hey, my aeroplane's got four wings," said Tim.

"Mine hasn't got any," said Tom.

"Mine's got four engines," said Tim.

"Mine must be a glider," said Tom.

Then they realised that they had got the parts of the two kits muddled up and the only thing to do was to pull them to pieces and start again.

- Use the model below to help you write your own short dialogue.

Write a short paragraph to introduce the dialogue.

" "
, said (name A) .

" "
, said (name B) .

" "
.

" "
.

Write a short paragraph to say what happens next.

Dear Helper,

Objective: to write own passage of dialogue, using reading as a model.

Talk about the example with your child to help them understand the reason for the punctuation and indentations. Discuss what their own dialogue might be about.

Name:

Once upon a time

A long time ago, something so strange happened that you'll never believe it.

Deep in his dreams, Robert heard his sister's voice and began to wake himself up.

The house was empty. The door was nailed up and the empty window frames banged in the wind. It was spooky.

Sally lived with Auntie May and her two cats. She was a shy little girl who liked to sit quietly and read books.

Once upon a time, there was a poor widow who had three sons. "I have nothing to give you," she said to them. "You must go and seek your fortune elsewhere."

"Aaah – it's an alien!" screamed Joanne.

- Read these story openings and talk about what kind of story they might lead into.
- Add some more story openings in the blank boxes.

Dear Helper,

Objective: to investigate sentences for story openings.

Discuss these story openings with your child. Talk about what kinds of a stories they might lead into. Help your child to find – or make up – more openings.

PHOTOCOPIABLE

T

Name:

Happily ever after

I hope you enjoyed my story – but I told you that you'd never believe it!

Robert woke up at last. "It was just a dream after all! I thought I woke up, but that was all part of the dream!"

The house was beautiful again. It had a new roof and windows, and the lawn was neatly mowed. It wasn't spooky anymore.

"That was quite an adventure for a shy person like me," thought Sally as she settled down to read a book.

The prince knocked on the door of the little cottage and an old woman answered it. "Don't you recognise me?" asked the prince. "I am your son!"

"It all goes to show," said Darren, "how the imagination can play tricks when it's dark!"

- Read these story endings and talk about what kind of story might have led up to them.
- Add some more story endings in the blank boxes.

Dear Helper,

Objective: to investigate sentences for story endings.

Discuss these story endings with your child. Talk about what kinds of a stories might have led up to them. Help your child to find – or make up – more endings.

Name:

T

Homework poem

- This homework poem is built up by repeating the first line and adding different excuses. Read the poem, then add some more excuses.

I didn't hand my homework in because
 I forgot it.
I didn't hand my homework in because
 I thought I had to hand it in tomorrow.
I didn't hand my homework in because
 It blew away on the way to school.
I didn't hand my homework in because
 My dog chewed it up.
I didn't hand my homework in because
 My mum couldn't do it.
I didn't hand my homework in because

I didn't hand my homework in because

I didn't hand my homework in because

I didn't hand my homework in because

I didn't hand my homework in because

- On a separate piece of paper, write another poem based on repeated lines, for example:

 I was late for school because...
 The funniest thing I ever saw was...
 School dinners remind me of...

Dear Helper,

Objective: to use repetitive phrases as the basis for writing poems.
Help your child to brainstorm ideas for this poem and for their own poem. Discuss how to sort the ideas into the most effective order.

T

Name:

Knock, knock

- Read these 'Knock, knock' jokes.
- Look at the way they are set out and discuss how they are similar to poems.

Knock, knock,
"Who's there?"
"Olive."
"Olive who?"
"Olive here, so let me in!"

Knock, knock,
"Who's there?"
"Frank."
"Frank who?"
"Frankenstein."

Knock, knock,
"Who's there?"
"Wilma."
"Wilma who?"
"Wilma supper be ready soon?"

- Write some of your own 'Knock, knock' jokes on the back of this sheet.

Dear Helper,

Objective: to design simple patterns with words.
Enjoy these 'Knock, knock' jokes with your child. Help them to think of other examples.

Name:

T

Shape up!

A **calligram** is a word or poem that is written in a way that shows its meaning. Here is an example:

Friendly Warning

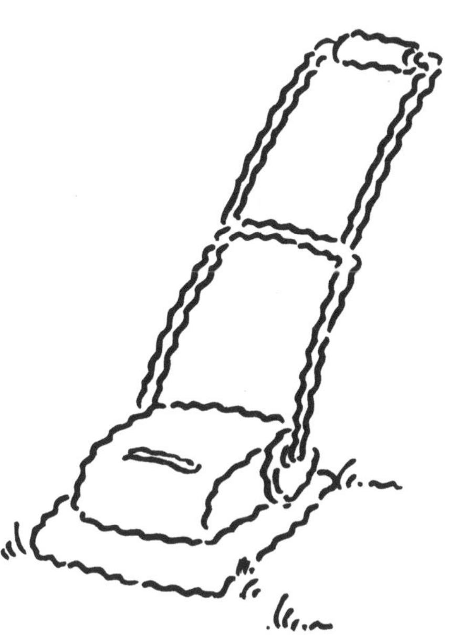

LISTEN GRASS, TAKE
IT EASY. DON'T GROW
TOO TALL. THEY'LL JUST
BRING IN A LAWN
MOWER AND CUT
YOU DOWN SHORT.

SEE? I TOLD YOU THEY WOULD.

Robert Froman

A **shape poem** is a poem in which the words are set out in a shape that fits the meaning of the words. Here is an example:

Mosquito

Mozzie

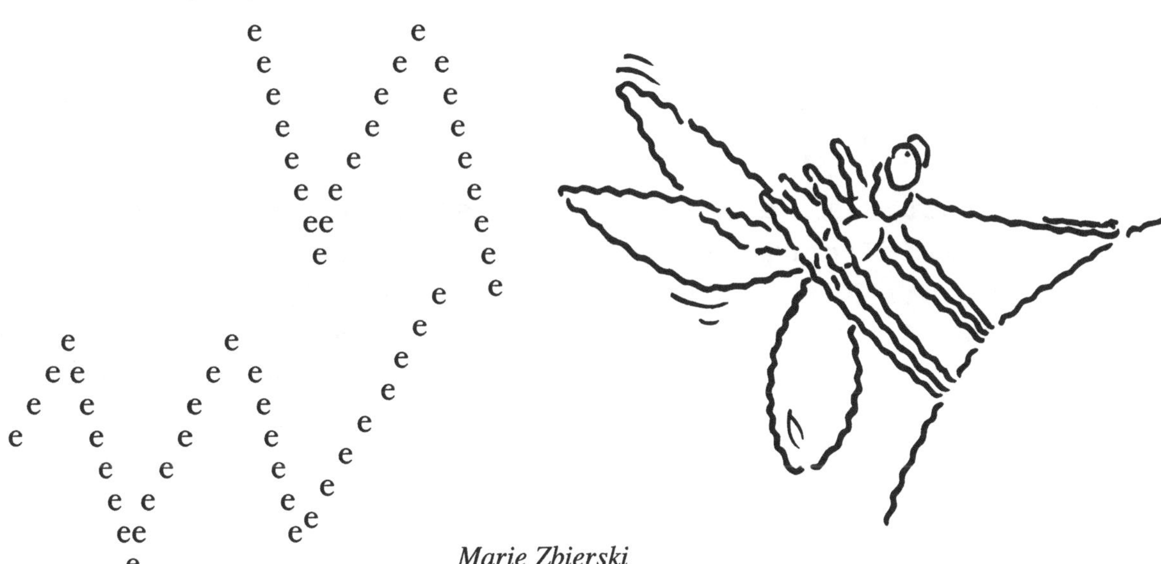

Marie Zbierski

- On a separate piece of paper, try some calligrams and shape poems for yourself.

Dear Helper,

Objective: to invent calligrams and a range of shape poems.
Have fun helping your child to invent calligrams and shape poems!

T

Name:

Bored boy

- Read this passage from *Schoolbot*, then turn it into a playscript using the example below as a starting point.

Bored with school, David sent a robot called Schoolbot in his place. The problem is, now he is bored with staying at home!

David, dozing in front of the TV, was woken up by Schoolbot coming home from school. "Good afternoon, David," said Schoolbot in his metallic voice.

"What's good about it?" said David grumpily.

"I thought you liked watching TV," said Schoolbot.

"It's all repeats," said David, flicking through the channels with the remote control. "I bet you had more fun at school!"

"Well, we had an interesting lesson on the addition of fractions..." began Schoolbot.

"Yuk!" David interrupted.

"...and a great game of football in which I scored 27 goals!"

David sighed. "I haven't played football for ages," he said sadly.

"Oh, and Karen asked me for a date."

David sat up suddenly. He was surprised to find that he felt jealous. "And what did you say?"

"I said that I didn't have any dates, but I was sure she could get them from the local supermarket."

Playscript starter

Schoolbot: (in a metallic voice) Good afternoon, David.

David: (grumpily) What's good about it?

Schoolbot: I thought you liked watching TV?

David: (flicking through the channels) It's all repeats. I bet you had more fun at school!

Extension

- On a separate piece of paper, finish the playscript for the scene.

Dear Helper,

Objective: to write a simple playscript based on a story.

Help your child to compare the story version with the sample of playscript, and then to complete the playscript, following the style.

Name:

T

Puppy problem

One way of indicating a new paragraph is to indent (move inwards) the first line from the margin.

- Use this paragraph plan to help you to write a story in paragraphs on a separate piece of paper.

Sam was a new puppy who had just come to live in Lucy's house.

(Describe Sam. What did he look like? What games did he like to play?)

Sam liked living in Lucy's house, but he kept getting into trouble.

(Describe some of the things he does wrong – for example, chewing cushions, getting mud on the carpet, or weeing in the house.)

Then one day, Lucy said, "You will have to go to school to be trained!"

(Describe how Sam is trained at dog school.)

When he had finished at school, Sam knew how to behave.

(Describe how Sam behaves after the training.)

After that, Sam managed to keep out of trouble – well, most of the time!

Dear Helper,

Objective: to use paragraphs in story writing.

Share ideas with your child about what might be written in each paragraph. When your child is writing the story, check that the rules of paragraphing are being followed correctly.

Name:

Fiction and non-fiction

- Cut out these book cover cards and sort them into fiction and non-fiction.
- Put the fiction into alphabetical order by author surname and non-fiction in alphabetical order by title. Paste the book covers down on a new sheet.

Dear Helper,

Objective: to understand the distinction between fiction and non-fiction.

Help your child to sort these books into fiction and non-fiction. Most are easy, but there are a couple that could be either. Discuss the categories in which these should be placed.

Name:

Fact or fiction?

- Below are the opening lines from eight books. After each one write whether it is **fact** or **fiction**. If you are not sure, write **unsure**.

Elizabeth I was the daughter of Henry VIII. She was born in 1533 and became queen of England in 1558. She died in 1603.

____

There was once a dog who had no home. His name was Sam. He was a mongrel, one of his ears was bitten off and he had a stumpy tail – which was probably why nobody wanted him.

____

This is the story of a ship called the *Titanic*, which sank below the freezing waves of the Atlantic in 1912.

____

Atlantis is a continent that used to be in the middle of the Atlantic Ocean. It was destroyed by an earthquake and sank below the waves thousands of years ago.

____

"Hey! Give me my pen back!" shouted Savi when he saw that Tim was using it.

"Be quiet!" ordered Miss Crotchet. "I want these notes finished by lunchtime!"

____

An escalator is a moving staircase. The first escalator was set up in Paris in 1900. Escalators normally move at a speed of 2mph.

____

Once upon a time, when dinosaurs roamed the Earth, a small lizard broke through its shell and entered the prehistoric world.

____

Fushun (pronounced foo-shun) is a coal-mining area in a remote part of China.

____

Dear Helper,

Objective: to understand the difference between fact and fiction.

Many of the book beginnings are easy to classify as fact or fiction, but your child will need to discuss some of them. For example, the last one sounds like a fact, but does Fushun really exist? How could you check it?

T

Name:

Crocodiles

- Compare these fiction and non-fiction passages and answer the questions below.

African Adventure

"Help!" shouted the boy.

He had been crossing the river when a crocodile had caught him by the foot. I ran to him and grabbed his arms and pulled as hard as I could. The boy screamed with pain. The crocodile glared at me with his tiny evil eyes. He thrashed his long grey tail to increase his pull, and I felt my grip slacken...

FICTION

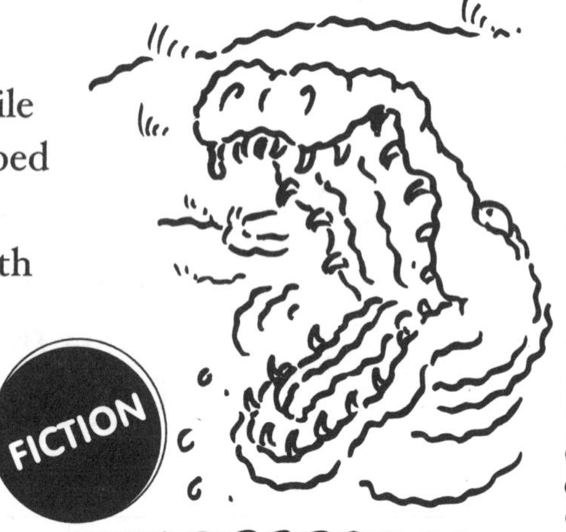

Crocodiles

Crocodiles are reptiles. They are found in Africa, Asia, Australia and Central America. The largest is the Indian salt-water crocodile which can grow up to 7 metres in length. Crocodiles move slowly on land,

but quickly in water. They have 30 to 40 teeth in each jaw. They are meat eaters and will sometimes attack humans. The female crocodile lays about 20 or 30 small white eggs.

- Which passage, fiction or non-fiction, gives the most realistic description of the crocodile?
- Which passage is the most exciting to read? Why?
- What are the differences in the way the two passages are set out?

Dear Helper,

Objective: to notice differences in the style and structure of fiction and non-fiction.

Read these two passages with your child and discuss the questions.

Name:

King Arthur

- Compare and discuss these two information texts.

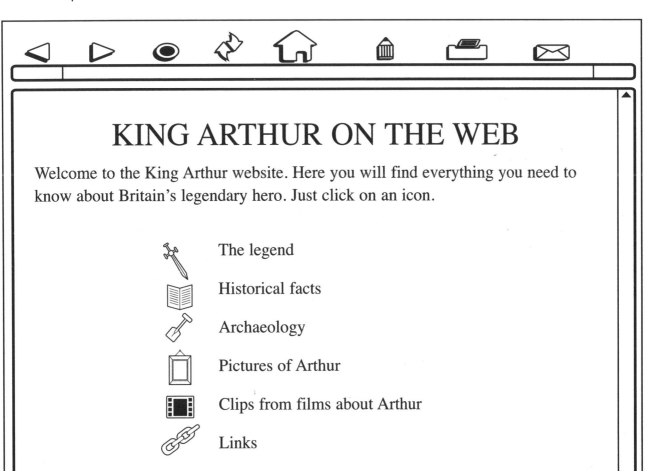

KING ARTHUR ON THE WEB

Welcome to the King Arthur website. Here you will find everything you need to know about Britain's legendary hero. Just click on an icon.

- The legend
- Historical facts
- Archaeology
- Pictures of Arthur
- Clips from films about Arthur
- Links

THE LEGEND OF ARTHUR

In the 5th century AD, Britain was invaded by Anglo-Saxons. The Britons fought back, and legend tells us that they were led by someone called Arthur. However, the Arthur of history would not have worn shining armour or lived in a huge castle. He would have worn the simple dress of a Celt and lived in a hill fort.

Dear Helper,

Objective: to compare a variety of information texts including computer-based sources.

Read these two texts with your child and discuss them. Both show only the beginnings. What would come next? How would the reader of the book find information on other aspects of King Arthur? What are the advantages and disadvantages of each type of information source?

PHOTOCOPIABLE

Name:

Hurricane

- Read this information about hurricanes and underline four key points.
- Write them out in the space below.

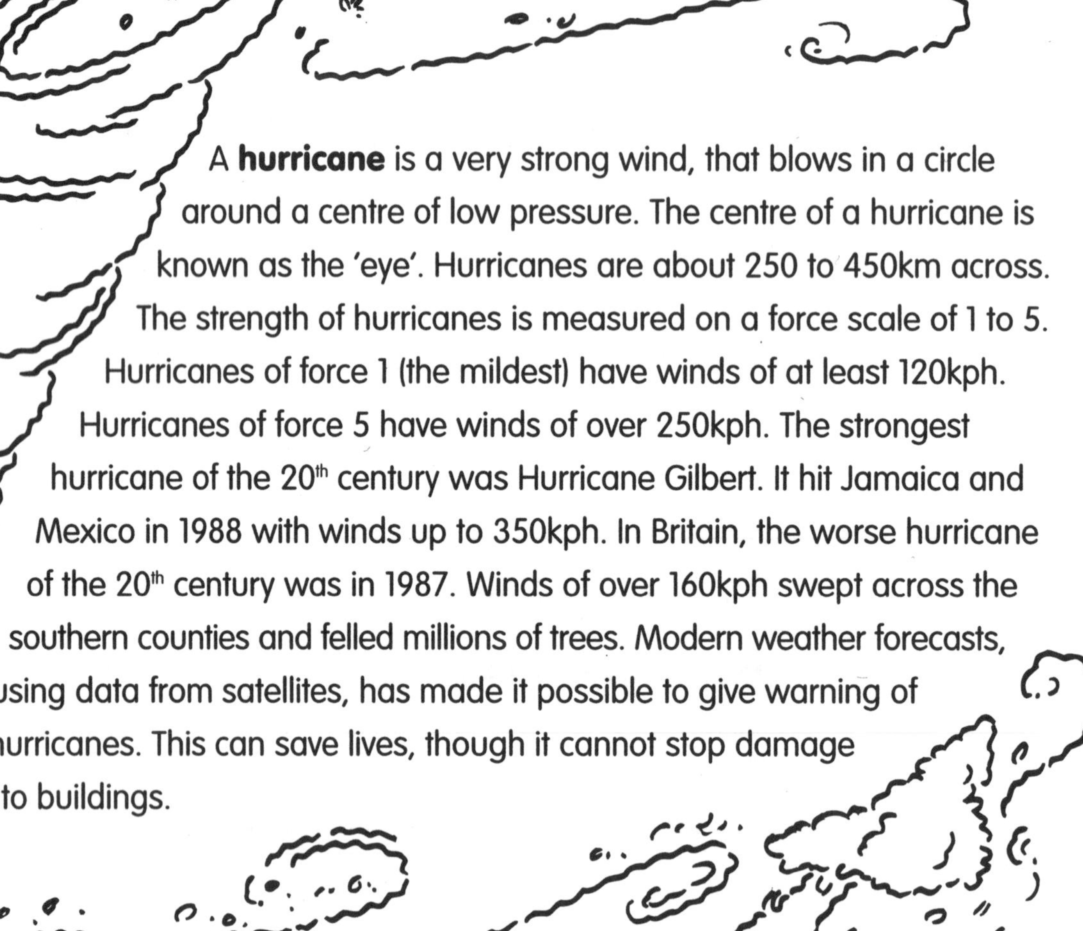

A **hurricane** is a very strong wind, that blows in a circle around a centre of low pressure. The centre of a hurricane is known as the 'eye'. Hurricanes are about 250 to 450km across. The strength of hurricanes is measured on a force scale of 1 to 5. Hurricanes of force 1 (the mildest) have winds of at least 120kph. Hurricanes of force 5 have winds of over 250kph. The strongest hurricane of the 20th century was Hurricane Gilbert. It hit Jamaica and Mexico in 1988 with winds up to 350kph. In Britain, the worse hurricane of the 20th century was in 1987. Winds of over 160kph swept across the southern counties and felled millions of trees. Modern weather forecasts, using data from satellites, has made it possible to give warning of hurricanes. This can save lives, though it cannot stop damage to buildings.

1 ______________________________

2 ______________________________

3 ______________________________

4 ______________________________

Dear Helper,

Objective: to identify the main points in an information passage.

Read the passage with your child and help them to pick out four key points. These should be the four most important facts.

Name:

W

Turbo trouble

- Look carefully at the picture, then write a report on the car. Fill in the table in note form, and write **P** (pass) or **F** (fail) at the end of each line.
- In the text box, put the information from the table into sentences.

Car Report

Make:		**Model:**
Part	**Comment**	**P or F**
Tyres		
Lights		
Wipers		
Bodywork		
Exhaust		
Other		
Text		

Dear Helper,

Objective: to write simple non-chronological reports from known information.

Help your child to find the faults in the car. Encourage them to be specific when writing about the faults, eg 'crack on passenger side of windscreen'. Most help will be needed when writing the information in sentences.

W

Name:

Adding -er and -est

- Complete the grid below by adding **-er** and **-est** to the words in the first column. Remember to apply these rules:

  Most words add -**er** and -**est** without change: able, abl**er**, abl**est**.

  Words ending in **e** drop the **e**: blue, blu**er**, blu**est**.

  Words with a short vowel before the consonant double the consonant: fat, fa**tter**, fa**ttest**.

  Words ending in **y** change **y** to **i**: smoky, smok**ier**, smok**iest**.

Word	Word +er	Word +est
big		
cloudy		
cold		
dry		
easy		
eerie		
high		
hot		
late		
low		
pretty		
red		
ripe		
slim		
small		
yellow		

Dear Helper,

Objective: to learn how words change when *-er* and *-est* are added.
Go over the spelling rules with your child and check that they apply them correctly.

Name:

Adding -s

activities	cats	half	scarves
armies	cities	inches	shelves
babies	clocks	kisses	spies
berries	countries	knives	telephones
bodies	dishes	lamps	televisions
books	dogs	leaves	thieves
boxes	elves	loaves	trenches
bushes	enemies	pencils	waltzes
calves	foxes	pennies	watches
carpets	glasses	pictures	wolves

- Cut out the word cards, then sort them into four groups to match the four ways of adding **s** listed below.

  Most words add **s** to make the plural: pack → pack**s**.

  Words that end in **s**, **ss**, **sh**, **ch**, **x** and **z**, add **es**: wish → wish**es**.

  Words ending in **y** change to **ies** if the **y** follows a consonant: belly → bell**ies**.

  Some words ending in **f** change the **f** to **ves**: self → sel**ves**.

Dear Helper,

Objective: to learn basic rules for changing the spelling of nouns when s is added.

This is a simple sorting exercise to help your child investigate four of the most important changes to words when s is added. All the words are 'regular', ie none are exceptions to the rules. Help your child to start the sorting exercise, then let them continue unaided.

W Name:

The silence of 'lamb'

- Every word below contains one or more silent letters. Say each word aloud, clearly but naturally, and listen carefully to the sounds you can hear. Find the silent letters in each word and underline or highlight them.
- Learn the spellings of these words, then test yourself with a partner or your helper.

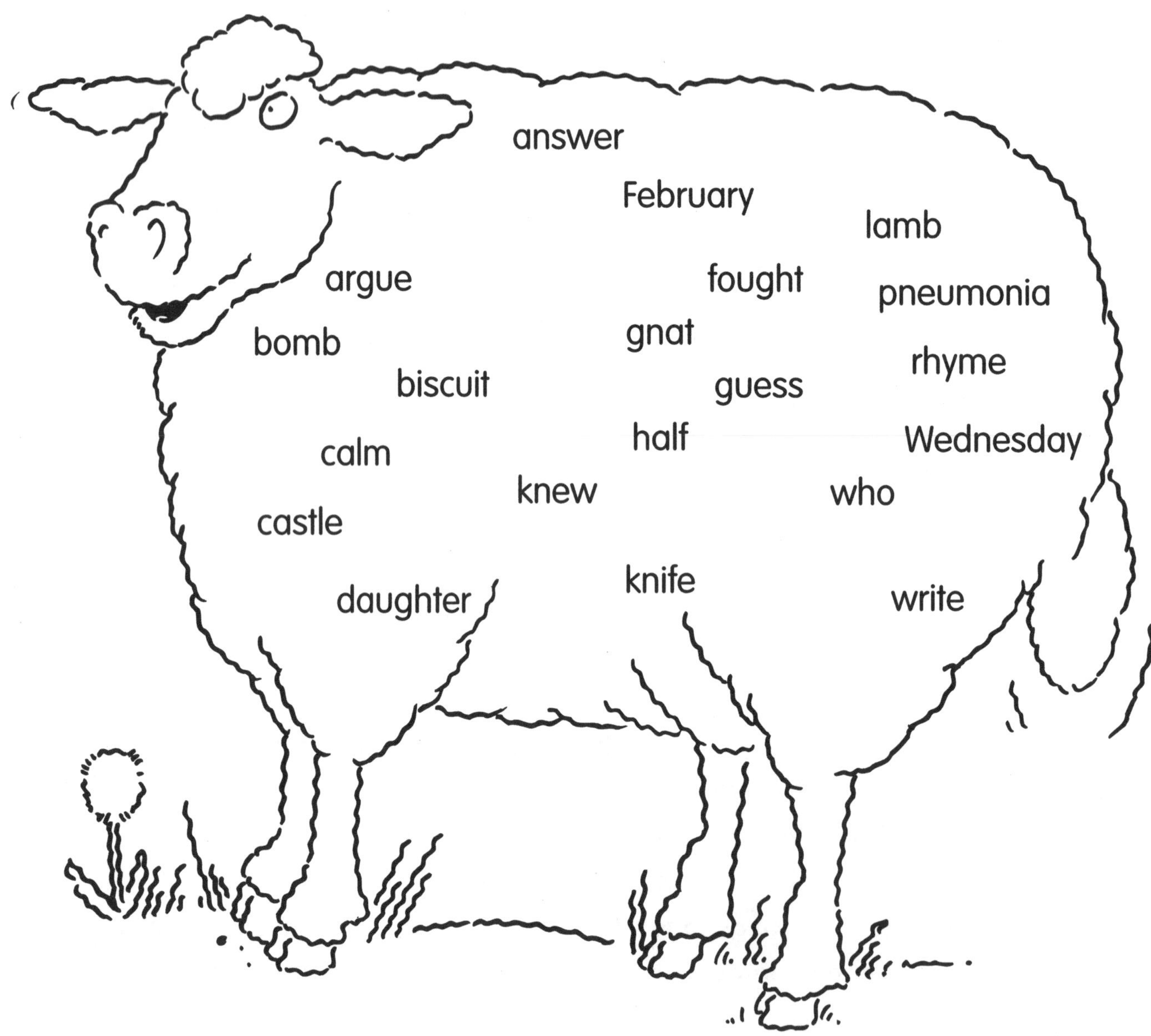

Dear Helper,

Objective: to investigate, spell and read words with silent letters.

Help your child to find the silent letters, then help them to learn the words. Give your child a test, but make it fun, and don't expect them to learn all the words at once!

Name:

W

A pair of trousers

Remember!
Singular means one of a thing. Plural means more than one.

- Sort these words into singular and plural. Write each one under the correct heading in the grid below.

trees shoes a pair of shoes flock
children bus sheep cassette
CDs flies fish dog
hippopotami calves trousers roof
cars potatoes giraffe zoo

Singular	Plural

Dear Helper,

Objective: to understand the terms singular and plural and to identify words appropriately.
Most of the words are easy to sort, but some will require extra thought. Discuss the more difficult words with your child.

Name:

The suffix kit

Nouns

ful	less	ly

Nouns

beauty	colour	hate	pity
boast	disgrace	joy	play
bottom	end	law	power
breath	faith	mercy	taste
care	fear	pain	tune
cheer	harm	peace	use

- Read this information about adding the suffixes -**ful**, -**less** and -**ly** to words.

  -ful makes a noun into an adjective meaning 'full of': hopeful = full of hope.

  Remember: 'full' as a word has two ls, but as a suffix it has only one l!

  -less makes a noun into an adjective meaing 'without': hopeless = without hope.

  -ly can be added after -full or -less to make an adverb (which describes how an action is done): hopefully, hopelessly.

  Remember: Some words can only be used with -ful or -less, not both!

  Words ending in y change y to i before adding a suffix.

- Now cut out the cards above. Make as many words as you can by combining the nouns and suffixes in different ways.

Dear Helper,

Objective: to recognise and spell common suffixes and understand how these influence word meanings.
Remind your child that a *suffix* is a word-part added to the end of a word to change its meaning. Help your child by checking that they understand the guidance.

Name:

Multi-purpose suffixes

These suffixes are often used to make up new words:

Suffix	Meaning	Example
-able	able to be	kissable
-agram	comes dressed up to your door	gorillagram
-athon	long, hard work	marathon
-cred	a good reputation in	street-cred
-friendly	liking or acting favourably towards	girl-friendly
-hostile	disliking or acting unfavourably towards	school-hostile
-ise/ize	makes a noun into a verb	hospitalise
-less	without something	brainless
-phobia	fear of	arachnaphobia
-speak	a way of speaking	edu-speak

- Look at these examples of new words, and then make up some of your own.

New word	Meaning
homeworkathon	lots and lots of homework
schoolphobia	fear of school
teacherise	make a person into a teacher

Dear Helper,

Objective: to use knowledge of suffixes to generate new words.

Remind your child that a *suffix* is a word-part added to the end of a word to change its meaning. Go over the suffixes and their meanings, then help your child to brainstorm new words using the suffixes.

PHOTOCOPIABLE

Name:

Don't do it!

cannot	can't
who has	who's
do not	don't
he had	he'd
are not	aren't
might have	might've
we will	we'll
of the clock	o'clock
Tom is	Tom's
will not	won't
should not	shouldn't
I am	I'm

Who's been sleeping in my bed?

I can't see a thing

- Read this information about using apostrophes.

  An apostrophe (') is used to show where a letter or letters have been missed out when words are shortened: do not → don't.

  Shortened forms (contractions) are best used for dialogue and informal writing such as diaries and personal letters.

- Now cut out the cards at the top of the page. Shuffle them and match the long forms with the short forms.
- Write out the short forms on a separate sheet.

Dear Helper,

Objective: to use the apostrophe to spell shortened forms of words.

After the matching game, read out some of the long forms and ask your child to write the shortened form. Check that they have spelled the word correctly and put the apostrophe in the right place.

Name:

W

Excel scientific instruments

- Read this advertisement and see if you can work out the difficult words from their context (that is, the words around them).

The Excel Company

The Excel Company manufactures and sells a wide range of scientific instruments. Our stethoscopes are so sensitive that a doctor can hear even the faintest sounds within the patient's chest. We also sell a barometer that measures air pressure very accurately - so accurately that some weather forecasters use it. Our theodolite is the first choice of surveyors. It enables them to measure angles and distances precisely, and helps them to plan better roads. We are particularly proud of our chronometers that measure time with an accuracy of plus or minus only a 60th of a second a year. Our electroencephalograph is preferred by many hospitals because of the accuracy with which it measures activity in the brain. If you make a purchase from us, you are sure to be satisfied as all our products come with a one-year warranty.

- Complete the glossary below. Then check your definitions using a dictionary.

	Glossary
barometer	
chronometers	
electroencephalograph	
manufactures	
products	
purchase	
stethoscopes	
theodolite	
warranty	

Dear Helper,

Objective: to figure out the meaning of unknown words from context.
Careful reading of the text will suggest an explanation of the difficult words. Your child should write their best guess in the glossary, then check it against a dictionary.

Name:

CD collection

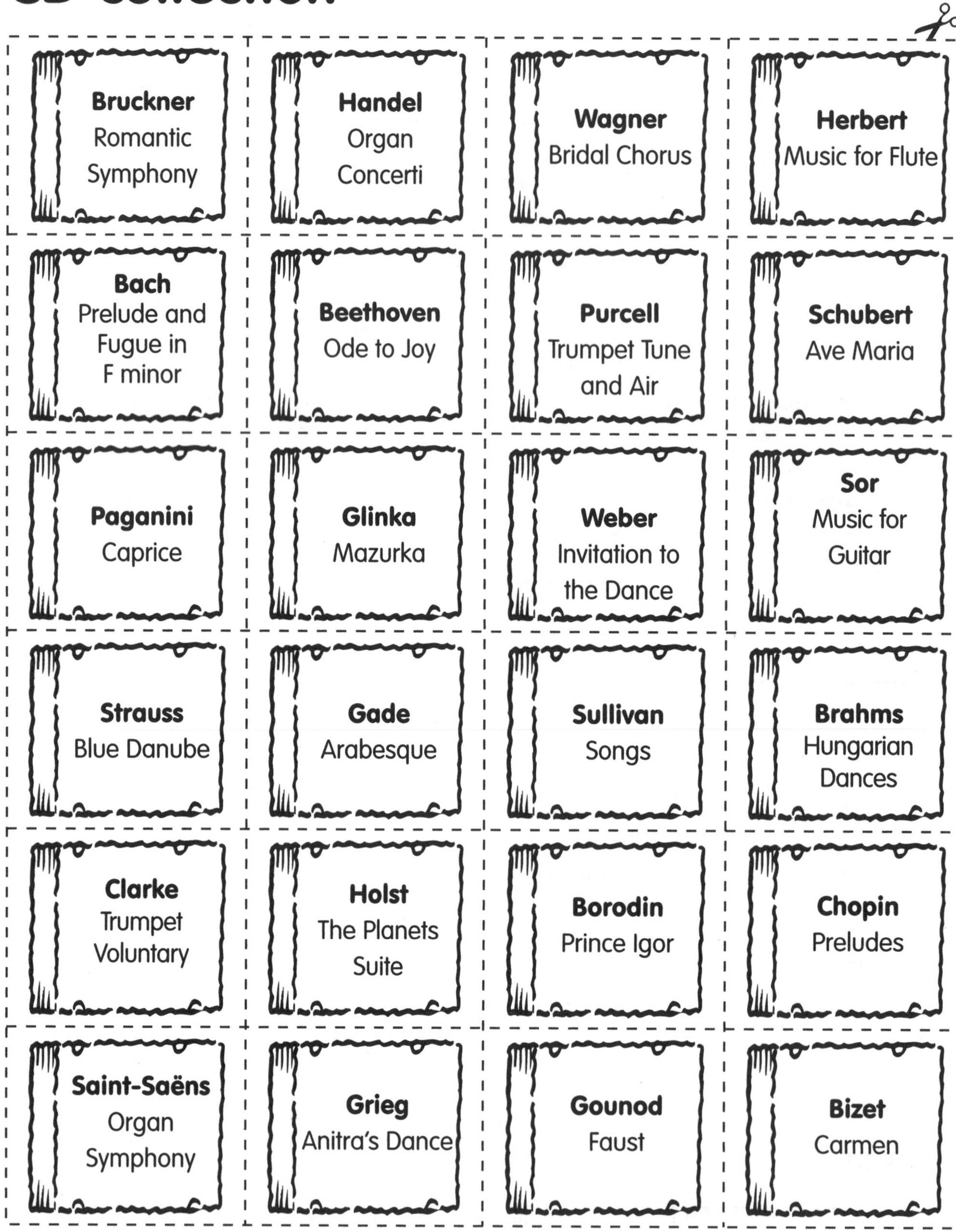

Bruckner
Romantic Symphony
Handel
Organ Concerti
Wagner
Bridal Chorus
Herbert
Music for Flute
Bach
Prelude and Fugue in F minor
Beethoven
Ode to Joy
Purcell
Trumpet Tune and Air
Schubert
Ave Maria
Paganini
Caprice
Glinka
Mazurka
Weber
Invitation to the Dance
Sor
Music for Guitar
Strauss
Blue Danube
Gade
Arabesque
Sullivan
Songs
Brahms
Hungarian Dances
Clarke
Trumpet Voluntary
Holst
The Planets Suite
Borodin
Prince Igor
Chopin
Preludes
Saint-Saëns
Organ Symphony
Grieg
Anitra's Dance
Gounod
Faust
Bizet
Carmen

- Organise these CDs into alphabetical order by composer.

Dear Helper,

Objective: to organise words or information alphabetically using the first two letters.
Help your child with the pronunciation of the composers' names, and keep a check on alphabetical order.

Name:

S

An alphabet of my dislikes

- Read this alphabet poem, then finish it off. Remember to give a reason for each dislike.

Aardvarks annoy me
Because they're first in the dictionary but I've never seen one.
Bullies upset me
Especially when they pick on me.
Computers frustrate me
'Cause they keep crashing.
Dinosaurs do nothing for me
But they're on TV all the time these days.
Eels make me feel all squirmy
Because they're so slimy and wriggly.
Fish for dinner is a turn-off
Because it's got bones in.

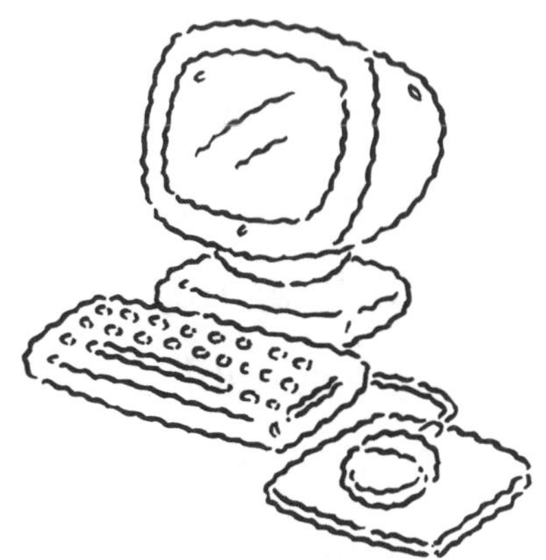

G

H

I

J

K

(Continue to **Z** on the back of the sheet.)

Dear Helper,

Objective: to organise words alphabetically.
Brainstorm ideas with your child about how to complete this alphabet poem. Browse through a dictionary for ideas, particularly for the difficult letters such as Q, X, Y and Z.

Name:

Opposite story

- Rewrite this story making every word in bold into an opposite word that *fits* the story. See how well Danny does then!

Friday was a **sunny** day, which always made Danny feel **happy**. He got out his bicycle and pedalled **quickly** to school. He did not want to be **late** because today he was going to get his test results.

"Good morning, Danny," said the teacher. "**Early** again, I see. **Good** boy! I will see that you get a suitable **reward**!"

Danny was very **pleased** and **smiled** at the teacher.

"You will not be surprised when I tell you that the **lazy** children have done **worst**," announced the teacher. "I will read the list of marks from the **bottom upwards**."

He picked up the list and started to read. "**Last** was William with 49 marks..." The teacher droned on through the list. "...And I am **pleased** to announce that Danny was **first**." The teacher **beamed** at Danny. "**Well** done, Danny. You are **top** of the class!"

The next lesson was RE, with a visiting vicar. The vicar's words made Danny feel **less** confident: "My text today," said the vicar, "is, 'the **first** shall be **last** and the **last** shall be **first**'."

Dear Helper,

Objective: to explore opposites.

Read through this story with your child. Ensure that they are able to put in suitable opposites verbally before writing out the 'opposite' version of the story.

Name:

Think of an adjective

- Look at the pairs of pictures, then fill in each space with an adjective that brings out the difference as much as possible.
  Remember to change **a** to **an** if necessary.

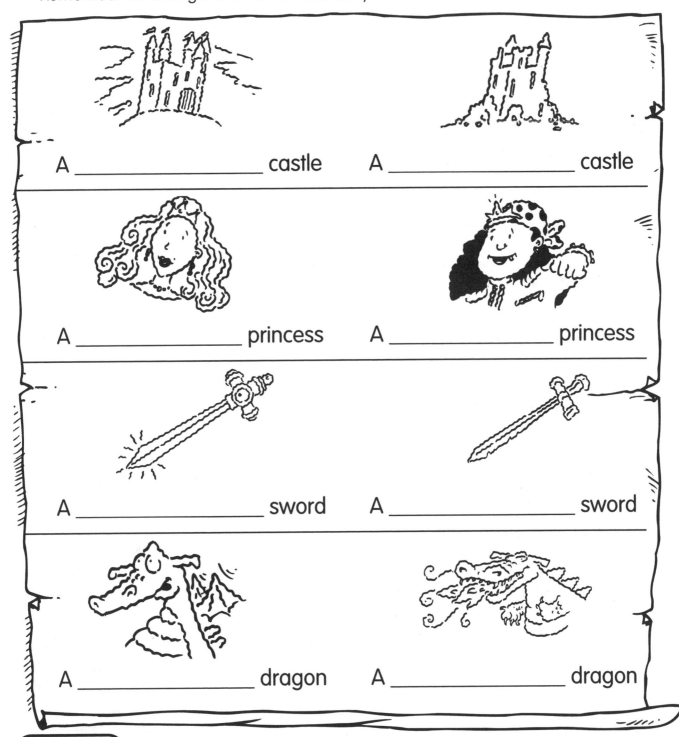

A ________________ castle A ________________ castle

A ________________ princess A ________________ princess

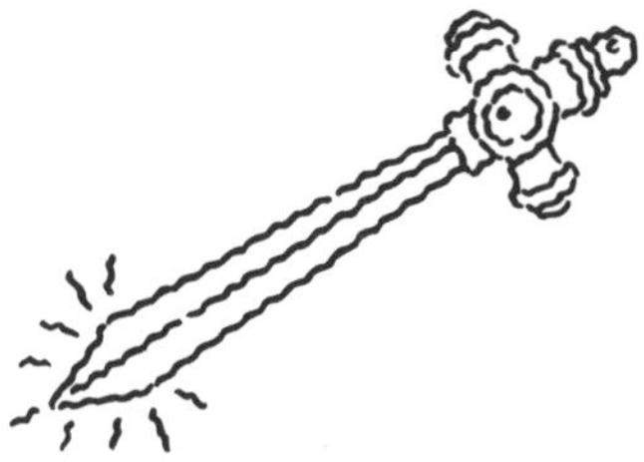

A ________________ sword A ________________ sword

A ________________ dragon A ________________ dragon

Dear Helper,

Objective: to experiment with deleting and substituting adjectives.

Encourage your child to try out different adjectives verbally before choosing the one to write in the gap. Emphasise that since the nouns are the same in each pair of cards the adjective must do all the work in showing the difference.

Name:

Singular to plural

- Change these sentences from **singular** to **plural** by changing nouns, verbs, pronouns and other words where necessary. An example has been done for you.

The boy walks his dog.

The **boys walk their dogs**.

The ship hit the iceberg.

____

Her tooth hurts badly.

____

I can jump over the hurdle.

____

The knife was lying on the table.

____

She heard the echo in the cave.

____

The thief tried to rob the bank.

____

The sailor swam to the boat.

____

The horse is eating a raw carrot.

____

The cat chased the mouse through the house.

____

He washes the glass in the sink.

____

Dear Helper,

Objective: to change sentences from singular to plural.

Encourage your child to read the singular sentences aloud, and then to say the plural versions before writing them down. Even if your child does not fully understand the grammatical terms (noun, verb and pronoun), they should be able to hear what is correct and incorrect. Point out any words in the sentences that your child has forgotten to pluralise.

Name:

S

A gaggle of geese

A **collective noun** names a group of people or things: **a gaggle** of geese.

- Join each collective noun to the correct group of people or things. One has been done for you.

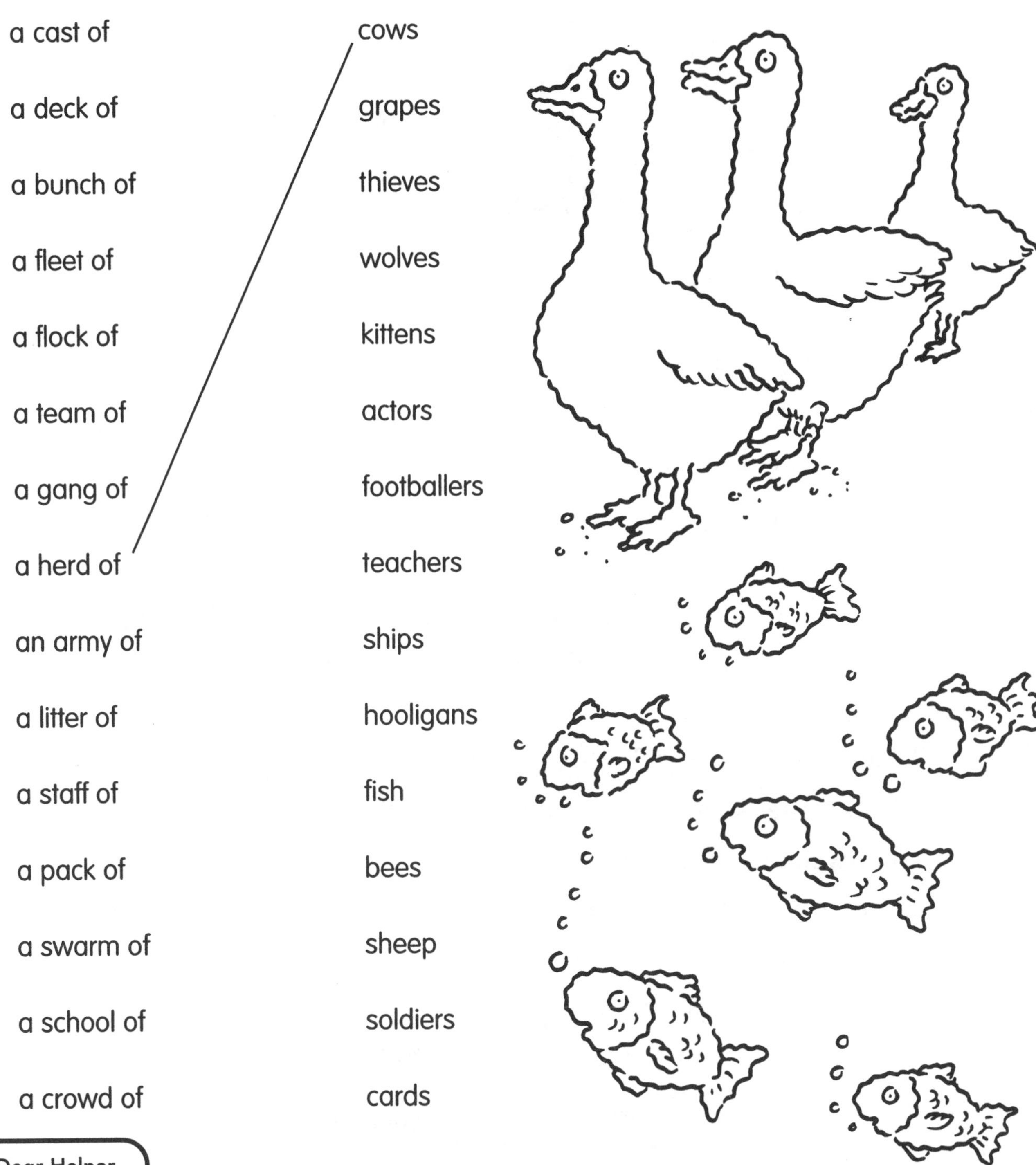

a cast of	cows
a deck of	grapes
a bunch of	thieves
a fleet of	wolves
a flock of	kittens
a team of	actors
a gang of	footballers
a herd of	teachers
an army of	ships
a litter of	hooligans
a staff of	fish
a pack of	bees
a swarm of	sheep
a school of	soldiers
a crowd of	cards

Dear Helper,

Objective: to understand what a collective noun is and to match collective nouns to their appropriate nouns.

Some of these collective nouns will be known to your child. Some may require your help. Encourage your child to make a guess and to use a dictionary, if one is available.

S Name:

How commas help

- Highlight or underline all the commas in the following text, then read it aloud.
- Talk about how commas make reading easier.

After their father is arrested, thirteen-year old Elinor is trying to hold the family together. Here, she is trying to cheer them up on a cold April day.

The weather turned colder. On 1 April, like a bad joke, there was a fall of hailstones, rattling against the windows and knocking over the daffodils. Then in the night it snowed, a wet, sloppy snow, already dripping down from the trees when they woke, and greying to slush on the pavements. Bambi had a bad cold.

"I hate this country," Sophia muttered.

"It'll be better soon," Elinor told her. "It'll be lovely next week, you'll see."

"Next week may be too late."

"Bambi's only got a cold. He won't die of it. He's getting better already. Wait till the sun comes out– "

"If it ever does," Sophia said gloomily.

"Wait and see," Elinor said, forcing herself to sound cheerful.

from *A Kind of Thief* by Vivien Alcock

PHOTOCOPIABLE

Dear Helper,

Objective: to note where commas occur in reading and discuss how they help the reader.
Listen to your child read this text, or share the reading. Talk about how commas help to make reading easier.

Name:

Schoolbot's poem

- Look at how capital letters are used in this text.
- Write each word with a capital letter in the correct column in the grid below. There is no need to write names more than once!

Schoolbot, the robot schoolboy, was working quietly in the library at Manor School.

"What are you doing, Schoolbot?" said Karen.

"Writing a poem with my new Bic ballpoint pen on this special Basildon Bond notepaper," he replied.

"Oh, please read it!" said Karen.

Schoolbot picked up the page and read:

"My love is like a red, red rose
"And that is why I love your nose.
"I also love your feet and toes
"And your pretty face..."

"Face doesn't rhyme," said Karen.

"I'm working on it," said Schoolbot, "and I expect that my Pentium 1000 brain will have the answer in no time."

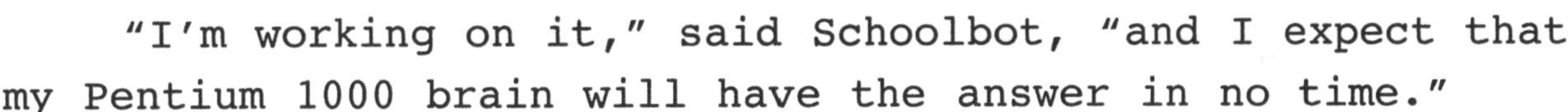

Name of person or place	To begin direct speech	Brand names	New lines in poetry

Dear Helper,

Objective: to identify the different uses of capital letters.

Help your child to identify each capital letter and to place the word in the correct column on the grid. It might help to highlight or underline them first in the text. Brand names may be particularly difficult to be sure of.

Name:

Let's get personal

The **person** of a verb is shown by the **personal pronoun** that goes before it. This table shows the different forms: first, second and third, singular and plural.

Personal pronouns

	Singular	Plural
First person	I	we
Second person	you	you
Third person	he/she/it	they

- Say which person (first, second or third) each of these texts is written in

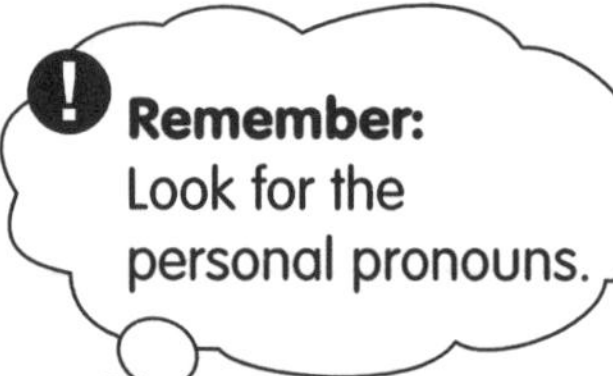

Remember:
Look for the personal pronouns.

Dear Diary
We had a great day today. We visited Conisbrough Castle. I really enjoyed the sound and light show, which told the story of the castle. I also enjoyed looking round the dungeon.

77 77 77
For really cheap telephone calls, dial 77 77 77! You do not need to change your telephone company, or have a new line installed. All you need to do is dial 77 77 77 and then the number.

Suki had never flown on a pterodactyl before. Her trainer had told her that it was like riding a horse – only more dangerous. She climbed into the saddle, took the reins; then, with a flick of the wrist, the great reptile rose into the air.

Dear Helper,

Objective: to show understanding of first, second and third person.

Help your child to identify which person each of these texts is written in. If they are able to do this quickly, look at a wide range of other texts in the home (eg instructions, cereal packets and stories) and talk about what person they are written in.

Name:

S

Let's agree

In sentences, the **subject** (what the sentence is about) and the **verb** (what the subject is doing) must **agree**.

The subject and verb must be identical in **number** (singular or plural) and in **person** (first, second or third).

- Each of the sentences below has two verbs (in bold). Put a ring around the verb that agrees with the subject.

Stephen **was/were** late for school.

Our cat and our dog **is/are** great friends.

I **is/am** first in the queue.

We **was/were** very tired after the party.

Each of the girls **is/are** going on holiday.

Neither Sally nor Amra **was/were** there at the time.

Both Tim and Tom **was/were** in trouble again.

All the children except Chloe **is/are** correct.

Dear Helper,

Objective: to understand the need for grammatical agreement in speech and writing.

Your child should be able to complete the first four sentences fairly easily. However, when working on the last four, ask your child to think carefully about whether the subject is singular or plural before choosing the singular or plural verb.

PHOTOCOPIABLE

Name:

Typical story language

- Here are some typical examples of story language found in folk and fairy tales. Think of some more examples (or find them in books) and write them on the back of this sheet.

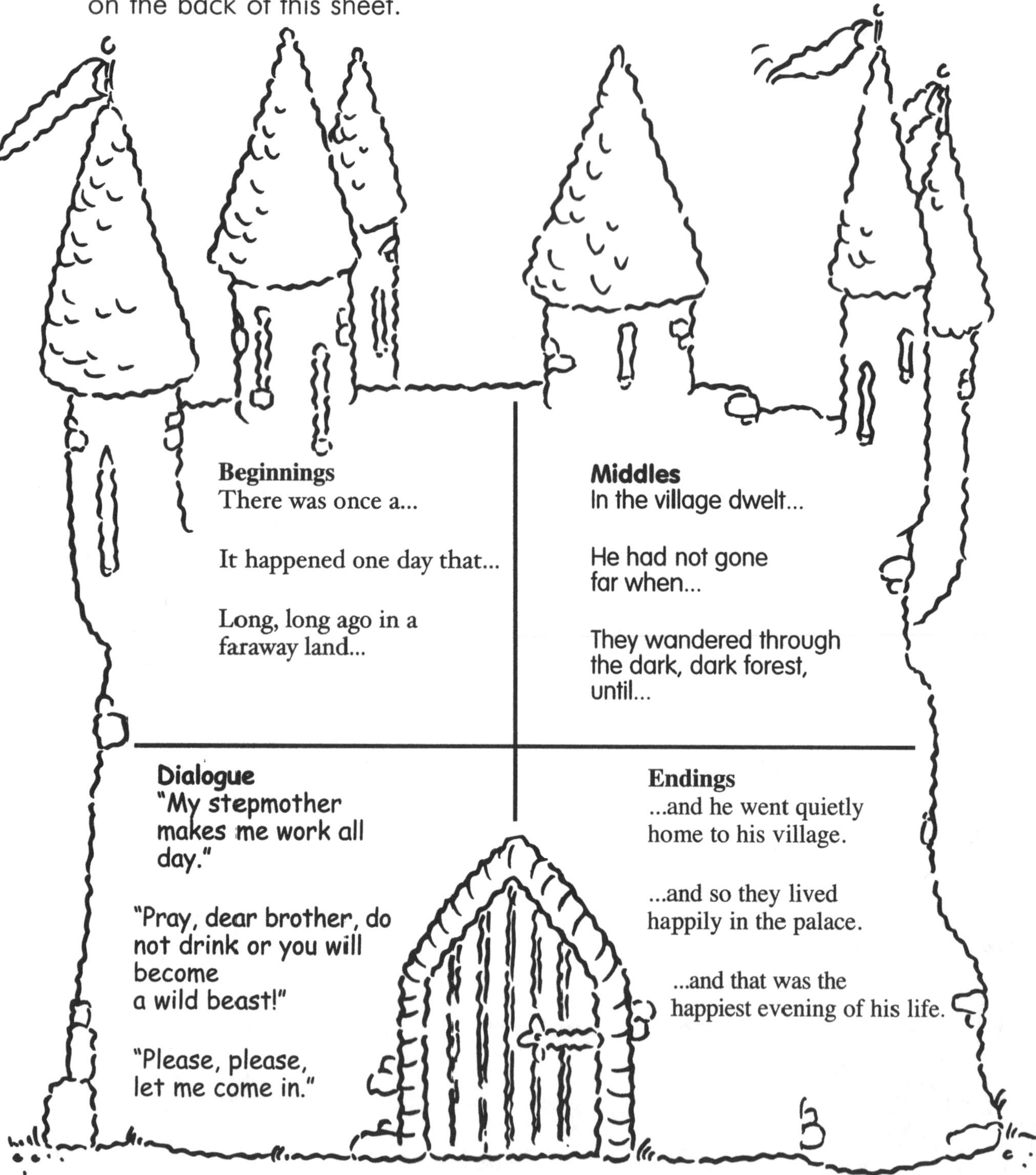

Beginnings
There was once a...
It happened one day that...
Long, long ago in a faraway land...
Middles
In the village dwelt...
He had not gone far when...
They wandered through the dark, dark forest, until...
Dialogue
"My stepmother makes me work all day."
"Pray, dear brother, do not drink or you will become a wild beast!"
"Please, please, let me come in."
Endings
...and he went quietly home to his village.
...and so they lived happily in the palace.
...and that was the happiest evening of his life.

- Now try to write your own story in the same style.

Dear Helper,

Objective: to explore the styles and voices of traditional story language.

Read through the examples with your child. Ask: 'Do you recognise them from any particular story?' Help your child think of – or find – other similar examples. Talk about how some of these phrases could be used in a story.

Name:

T

The choosing

- Read this story, then answer the questions.

There was once a young shepherd who wished to marry. He knew three sisters who were all equally pretty, so it was difficult for him to choose between them.

So he asked his mother for advice. She said, "Invite all three to our house and put some cheese on the table before them. Then watch how they eat it."

Next day, the young man invited the three sisters to his house and put a plate of cheese in front of each one. The first girl swallowed the cheese with the rind on. The second girl hastily cut the rind off the cheese, but she cut it so quickly that she left much good cheese with it, and threw that away as well. The third girl, however, peeled the rind off carefully, and wasted none of the cheese.

The young man asked his mother what she thought of the three girls. She replied, "Take the third for your wife."

This he did, and lived contentedly and happily with her.

The Brothers Grimm

- Why did the shepherd find it difficult to choose between the three sisters?

- What did the way they ate the cheese show about them?

- How do you think the shepherd should have found the most suitable girl?

- What kind of a wife do you think the third girl will be?

Dear Helper,

Objective: to identify typical story themes.

Share the reading of the story with your child, then discuss the theme by exploring situations where you or your child have had to make choices. What helped you to decide? Finally, discuss the questions in preparation for your child's written answers.

Name:

Emil

- Read this character description of Emil. Then answer the questions below.

Perhaps you will have already heard of Emil, who lived at Katthult in Lönneberga in Småland. You haven't? Well, well! But I can assure you there isn't a single person in Lönneberga who hasn't heard of that naughty little boy. He got into more kinds of mischief than there were days in the year, and frightened the people of the district so much that they wanted to send him far away from Sweden. They did, really! They collected a lot of money and took it to his mother and said, 'Maybe there's enough there to pay for sending Emil to America.'

They thought Lönneberga would be far more peaceful without Emil, and of course that was true, but Emil's mother was very angry indeed and flung the money all over the place.

'Emil's a dear little boy,' she said, 'and we love him just as he is.'

And Lina, the maidservant in Katthult, said, 'Besides, we ought to consider the Americans, too. They've never done us any harm; so why should we plague them with Emil?'

from *Emil Gets Into Mischief* by Astrid Lindgren

- Emil's actions are not described, so how do we know how naughty he is?

- What does Emil's mother think of him? Why do you think her feelings are different to everyone else's?

- What kind of things do you think Emil did to frighten people so much?

Dear Helper,

Objective: to explore and discuss a main character.

Read through this description with your child and talk about what it is that brings the character to life. Discuss answers to the questions, sharing your ideas as well. Ask: 'Would you like to know more about Emil? Why or why not?'

Name:

T

Dialogue Between Two Large Village Women

- Read this poem and perform it with a partner or your helper.

Dialogue Between Two Large Village Women

Vergie mi gal, yu know
wha overtek me?

Wha, Bet-Bet darlin?

Yu know de downgrow buoy
dey call Runt?

Everybody know de lickle
orceripe wretch.

Well mi dear, de bwoy put
question to mi.

Wha? Wha yu sey?

Yeahs – put question to mi
big-big woman, who could be
him mummah over and over.

Laad above. Didn yu bounce
de lickle ramgoat face?

Mi hol him an mi shake
de lickle beas like
to kill de wretch.
An yu know wha happen?

No.

De lickle brute try fi kiss mi.

James Berry

Dear Helper,

Objective: to choose and prepare a poem for performance.
Help your child with the phonetic pronunciation of the words, then take each part in turn.

Name:

Plot cards

- The cards below give six basic plots for a story. Talk about each of them, then choose one to develop into a story plan. (If you wish, adapt the ideas freely and use ideas from other cards.)

Dragon

A terrible dragon is destroying the countryside and eating maidens.
The king promises half his kingdom to anyone who can kill the dragon.
Many knights try to kill the dragon and fail. Describe what happens to one of them.
A poor boy/girl decides to have a go.

Three trials

A young man asks for a princess's hand in marriage, but her father says he must first pass three trials.
He undergoes three strange trials, with three clever ways to solve them. The princess could help him secretly.

Princess in disguise

There is a terrible monster that everybody is frightened of.
A knight is hired to kill the monster. He fights the monster, but just before he kills it, the monster asks for a kiss. Is it a trick?
Should the knight agree or should he kill the monster?
He kisses the monster and it turns into a beautiful princess.

Quest

Far away over the mountains is a fabulous treasure.
The hero/heroine has many adventures on the journey.
What do they find when they get there?
Is it what they expected?

Fortune seeker

A family is so poor the mother cannot afford to feed her children. She sends them out to seek their fortune.
Tell the story of each one.
The first two fail and the third succeeds.

Three wishes

The hero/heroine does a good deed one day, for example rescues a drowning cat.
In return, they are given three wishes.
Tell the story of each wish.
Do the wishes work out well or badly?

Dear Helper,

Objective: to plan main points as a structure for story writing.

Discuss these six plots with your child. During discussion, encourage them to elaborate by adding other ideas. Finally, your child should choose one of the plots and write their ideas as a detailed story plan. Encourage them to use ideas from other cards if they wish to.

Name:

T

Story game

- Turn a story into a board game. Write some of the main problems in squares with instructions such as: **Miss a turn** or **Go back two spaces**. Write some of the good things in the story in some squares with instructions like: **Take an extra turn** or **Move ahead one space**. Make counters for the main characters.

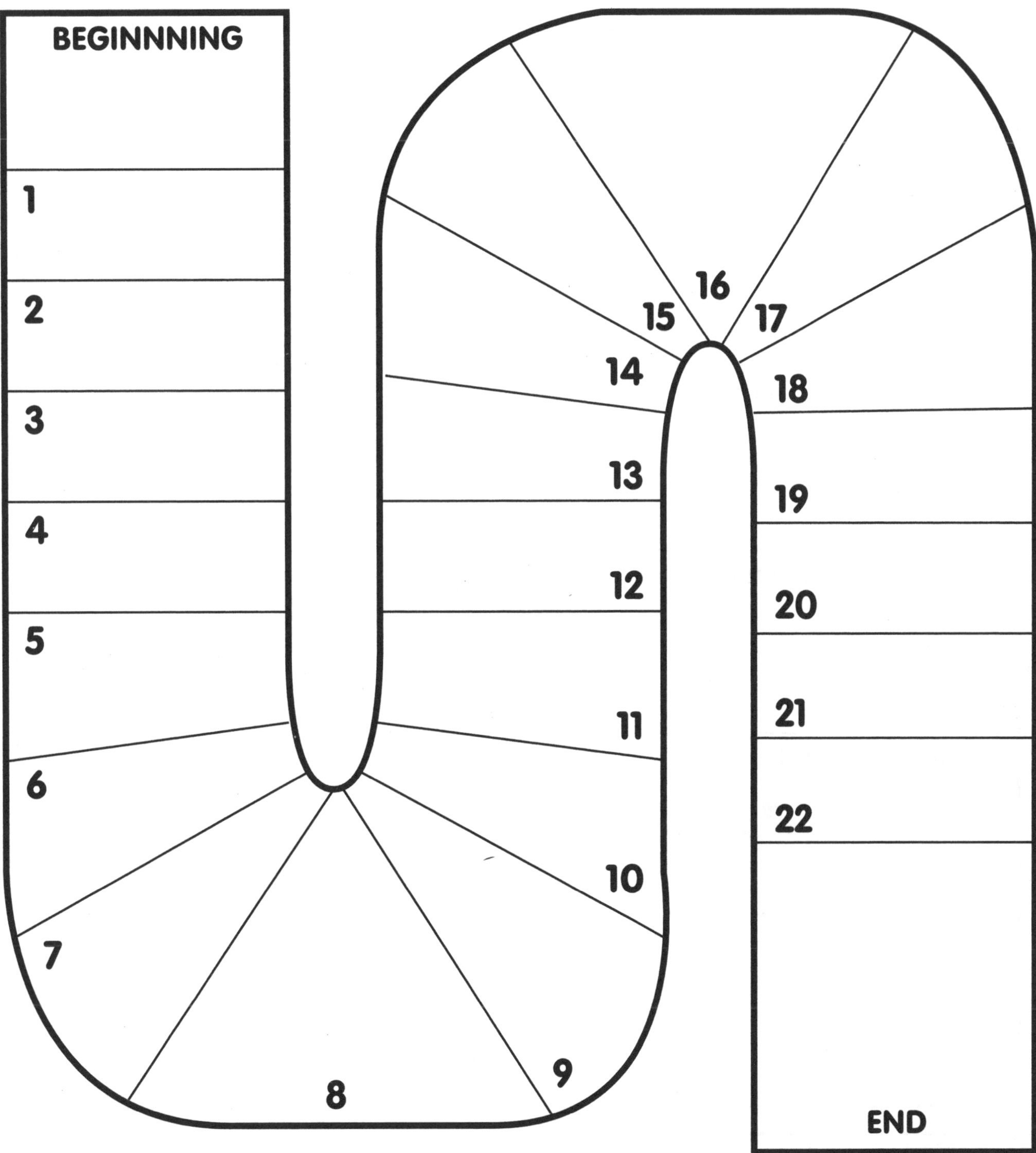

Dear Helper,

Objective: to describe and sequence key incidents in a variety of ways.

Your child will also bring home a story with this sheet. Help them to pick out key incidents from the story and place them on the blank game board. Play the finished game with your child.

T

Name:

Character card

- Write a reference card about a character in a book that you have been reading. Sketch a portrait in the picture frame.

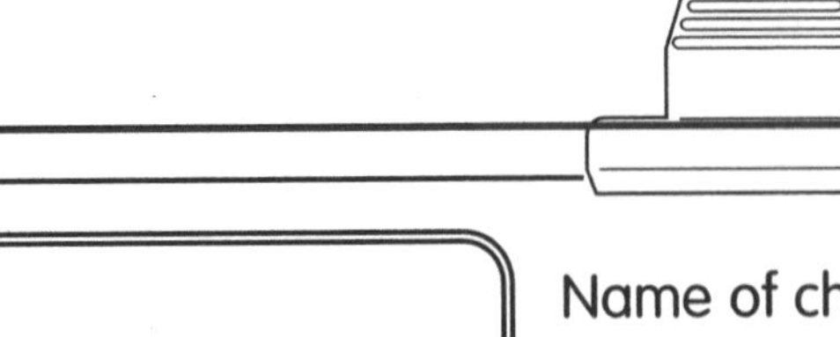

Name of character: ____________________

Title of book: ____________________

Description of character:

Some words or phrases quoted from the story to describe the character:

What the character does:

How the character changes throughout the story:

Dear Helper,

Objective: to write about a character from a story.

Your child will have brought home a story or notes for use with this activity. You can help by discussing each aspect of the character card with your child and looking for suitable evidence in the story.

Name:

T

How the elephant got a long trunk

- Read this well-known myth.

"Keep away from that lake, Ellie," said her mother. Now, Ellie the Elephant had not thought about the lake before, but suddenly it sounded interesting. When her mother wasn't looking, she decided to take a peek.

She found the lake and was disappointed. It was just like a large puddle after all. But all that walking had made her thirsty, so she decided to have a drink – she didn't know that Alligator was looking for food! Ellie dipped her short trunk into the water (in those days, all elephants had short trunks). Alligator thought that it was a fish, so he swam up and bit Ellie's trunk.

"Let go of my trunk! Let go of my trunk!" she shouted. But Alligator didn't hear and started pulling Ellie's trunk even harder. They both tugged and tugged and Ellie's trunk stretched and s-t-r-e-t-c-h-e-d!

After a while, Alligator gave up – this fish was too tough – and he went after a smaller fish that had just swum by.

Ellie's trunk was very sore – and very long. She felt silly at first, but soon found out how useful it was. She could pick things up with it, give herself a shower with it, and many more wonderful things. Of course, when Ellie grew up and had babies, they all had long trunks too – and this is how elephants got long trunks!

- Now plan a similar myth of your own. Here are some ideas:

How the mouse got a long tail
How the rabbit got big ears
How the crocodile learned to swim
How the parrot learned to talk
How the snake lost its legs

Dear Helper,

Objective: to write a story plan for a myth using a theme from one read.

Remind your child that a myth is a story that tries to explain something we don't understand or how something came to be. Share the reading of the myth with your child, then discuss ideas for writing a new myth of the same kind.

T

Name:

The sequel game

- Cut out the story cards, mix them up and lay them face down.
- Take it in turns with a partner to pick up a card and tell a sequel to the traditional story – a follow-on story that uses some of the same characters and settings. Do this several times.
- Then choose the idea you like best and make notes for a written story sequel.

Dear Helper,

Objective: to plan a sequel to a well-known traditional story.

Ensure your child is familiar with all the stories on the cards. If there are some that are unknown, discard these and only use the familiar ones. Encourage your child to base their sequel on some of the characters and settings from the original story, but to think about different plots.

Name:

Sequel planner

- Write notes about a story you have read in the **Story** column.
- Write a plan for a sequel in the **Sequel** column.

Story	**Sequel**
Title:	**Title:**
List the characters in the story. Add a phrase of description to each name.	Which characters will you use in the sequel? Will there be any new characters?
List the places in the story. Add a phrase of description for each place.	Will the sequel be set in one of the places in the story or will the characters go to a new place?
Write what happens at the end of the story.	What happens at the beginning of the sequel? Make sure it 'follows-on' from the story.

Dear Helper,

Objective: to write a sequel to a traditional story.

Your child should have brought home a story they have read, or notes, for use with this activity. Help them to use these to fill in the 'Story' column. Then share ideas for the sequel, filling in the right-hand column with the ideas you both agree are best.

Name:

Why?

- Perform this poem with another person. Then, on a separate sheet, add more verses following the same pattern. A good place to add the new verses would be before the last two lines.
- Try to write a completely new Why? poem, using the same pattern.

I'm just going out for a moment

I'm just going out for a moment.
Why?
To make a cup of tea.
Why?
Because I'm thirsty.
Why?
Because it's hot.
Why?
Because the sun is shining.
Why?
Because it's summer.
Why?
Because that's when it is.
Why?
Why don't you stop saying why?
Why?

Michael Rosen

PHOTOCOPIABLE

Dear Helper,

Objective: to write new verses for a given poem, following the same pattern.

Perform this poem with your child, then brainstorm ideas for new verses. Help your child to write a whole new poem on the same pattern.

Name:

Instructions

- Instructions serve many purposes. Look at these examples and write down what they are for.
- Collect more examples.

SAFETY NOTICE

If you hear seven short blasts on the ship's whistle you must go to the nearest **MUSTER STATION.** You will be given a lifejacket and told what to do next.

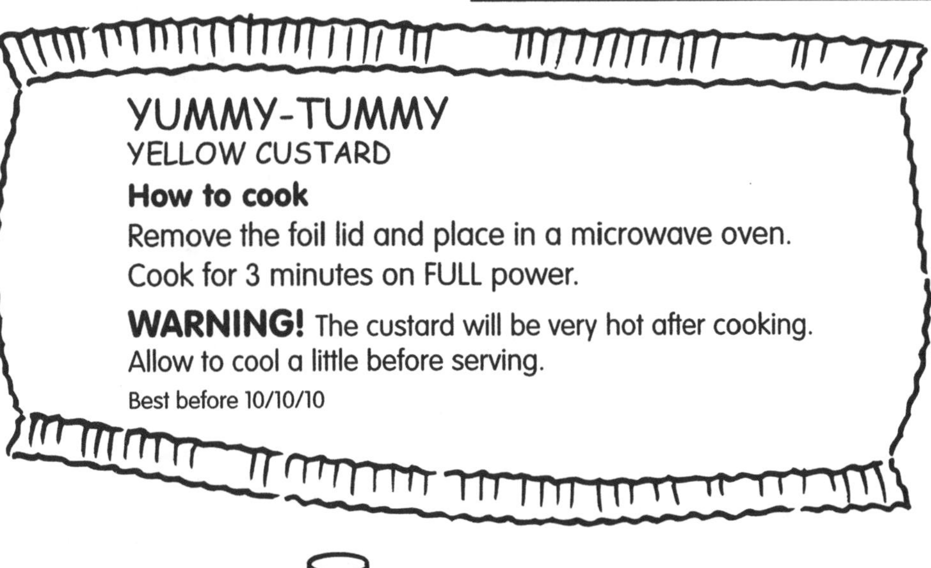

YUMMY-TUMMY
YELLOW CUSTARD
How to cook
Remove the foil lid and place in a microwave oven.
Cook for 3 minutes on FULL power.
WARNING! The custard will be very hot after cooking.
Allow to cool a little before serving.
Best before 10/10/10

Micklebring 2

Braithwell 4

Clifton 1

Dear Helper,

Objective: to identify the different purposes of instructional texts.

Help your child to find more examples of instructions – the house is probably full of them. For example, instructions for electrical appliances and cooking instructions on packets and in recipe books.

PHOTOCOPIABLE

T

Name:

New mini-system

- Read these instructions and highlight the following features: lists, numbered points, diagrams and bullet points.

WARNING!
To prevent fire or shock hazard,
do not expose the unit to rain or moisture.

Your retro 70s mini-system includes:

- 1 system box with CD player, cassette deck, radio and amplifier
- 2 teak-effect front speakers
- 4 speaker cables
- AM/FM antenna
- 1 remote control (and batteries)

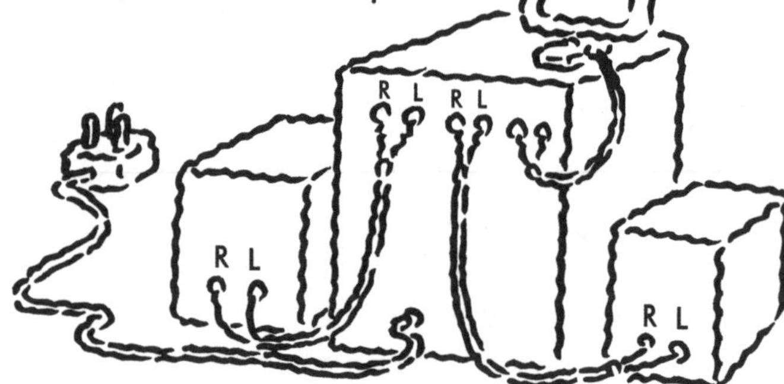

Setting up the system

1 Connect the speakers by placing the red wire in the red socket and the black wire in the black socket and closing the clips.

2 Connect the AM/FM antenna by placing the black wires in the black sockets and closing the clips.

3 Place the batteries in the remote control unit.

This mini-system has Dolby* B noise reduction.

* Dolby and the double-D symbol are trademarks of Dolby Laboratories Licensing Corporation.

PHOTOCOPIABLE

Dear Helper,

Objective: to explore how written instructions are organised.

Help your child to find the features listed in the note at the top of the page. If possible, do the same with a real instruction manual.

Name:

T

How to make a book

- Follow these instructions to make a 16-page mini-book.

You will need:
A sheet of A4 paper
A pair of scissors
A stapler

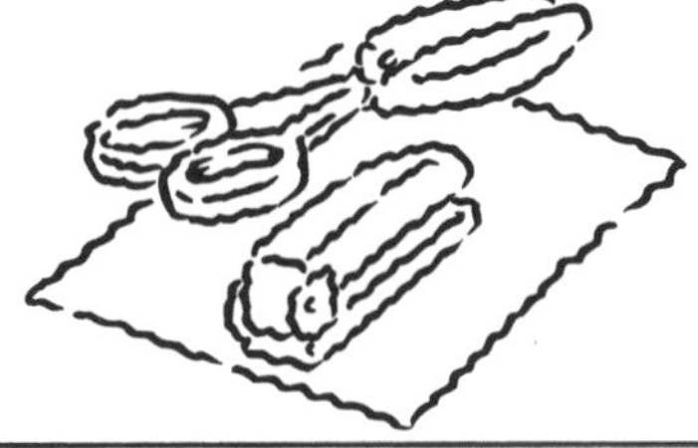

What to do:

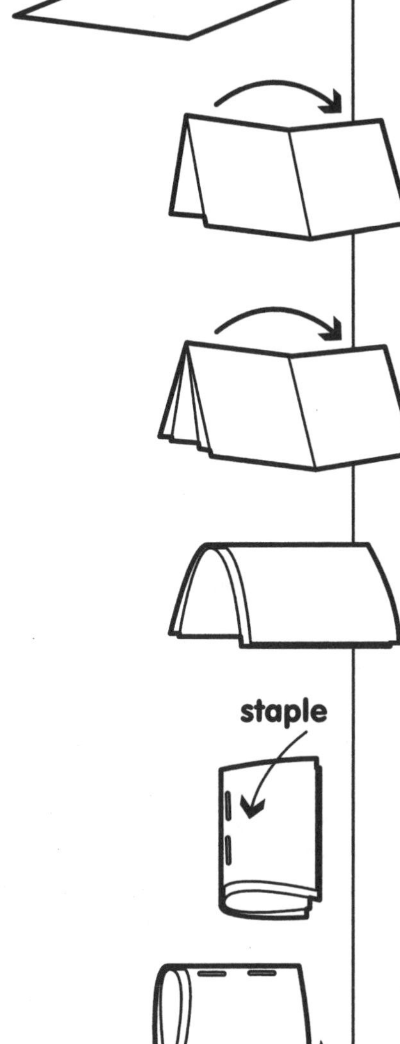

1 Take the sheet of A4 paper and fold in half, short side to short side.

2 Turn sideways so that the fold is at the top, then fold in half again as above.

3 Repeat step 2.

4 Turn the paper so that the all the folds are at the top and at the right-hand side.

5 Open out the paper once and staple through the fold.

6 Cut the folds along the top and along the right-hand side.

Your book is finished! Now you could write a story or a collection of poems to fill it.

Dear Helper,

Objective: to read and follow simple instructions.
Read through these instructions with your child, then supervise as they follow them. They are not expected, at this stage, to write a story or collection of poems!

T

Name:

How to make a recording

- Write instructions to make a recording. Use the objects in the picture and the framework below to help you.

You will need:

-
-
-
-

What to do:

1

2

3

4

5

PHOTOCOPIABLE

Dear Helper,

Objective: to write instructions.

Discuss with your child how to make a recording, then ask them to write instructions. Note that they can add extra bullet points and numbers if needed, and can also use the other side of the page.

Name:

T

Notes

- Read this encyclopedia entry about Galileo and the notes made about it.

Galileo was born in 1564 in Pisa, Italy. He was the first person to look at the night sky with a telescope. Through it he could see things that cannot be seen with the naked eye, such as the rings of Saturn and the moons of Jupiter. His book on astronomy was banned by the Church. He died in 1642.

Notes

Galileo, Italian
b. 1564
1st to use telescope
saw rings of Saturn,
moons of Jupiter
book banned by Church
d. 1642

- Now write your own notes for this entry about Herschel.

Herschel, Sir William, was born in 1738 in Hanover, Germany, but he spent most of his working life in England. In 1781 he discovered Uranus and some of its moons. He also discovered double stars and infra-red rays from the sun. He died in 1822.

Dear Helper,

Objective: to practise note-making.

Help your child to study the sample notes on Galileo. They should note how only the most important points are jotted down. They should then make similar notes on Herschel.

PHOTOCOPIABLE

W Name:

Words within words

Jobs	Insects	Flowers
butcher	butterfly	bluebell
carpenter	daddy-long-legs	carnation
engineer	dragonfly	dandelion
fisherman	earwig	honeysuckle
programmer	grasshopper	rhododendron

Birds	Fruit	Dogs
kingfisher	blackcurrant	Airedale
moorhen	gooseberry	bloodhound
nightingale	orange	bulldog
partridge	peach	Dalmatian
puffin	pineapple	sheepdog

Geography	Space	School
capital	atmosphere	blackboard
country	midnight	history
hillock	moon	mathematics
island	planet	poetry
plain	sunset	teacher

- Cut out these cards, shuffle them, and then deal out two cards to each player.
- Each player then has to see how many words they can find within the words on their cards.

Note: Consecutive letters only are allowed.
The same word is only counted once (for example, on the **Birds** card three of the words contain **in**, but it can only be counted once).

Dear Helper,

Objective: to identify short words within longer words.

Play this game several times with your child. Being able to identify short words within longer words is an aid to correct spelling.

Name:

W

Non-stick

The prefixes **non-**, **ex-**, **co-** and **anti-** are often used to make up new words. Here are some examples of recent words:

non- (means not)	**ex-** (means former)	**co-** (means joint)	**anti-** (means against)
non-fiction	ex-girlfriend	coeducation	antibiotic
non-smoker	ex-husband	co-star	antidote
non-stick	ex-policeman	co-worker	antifreeze

- Make up your own new words. Some starter ideas can be found below. Note that, although **smoker** works with all the prefixes, many words will only work with one or two prefixes.

Words to try	**Word + prefix**	**Meaning**
smoker	non-smoker	not a smoker
	ex-smoker	used to be a smoker
	co-smoker	smokes with somebody
	anti-smoker	against smokers
alien		
chocolate		
computer		
nuclear		
person		
reading		
school		
tangle		
teacher		
vegetable		

- Now think of some of your own words to add prefixes to. List them on a separate sheet.

Dear Helper,

Objective: to recognise and spell the prefixes *non-*, *ex-*, *co-* and *anti-*.

Remind your child that a *prefix* is a word-part added to the beginning of a word to change its meaning. Check that your child does not add prefixes in a thoughtless way. They must be able to say what the new words mean.

Name:

Pirate talk

- Highlight all the synonyms of **said** in this passage adapted from *Peter Pan*.
- On a separate sheet, list the synonyms and add any others you can think of.

Michael began to cry, and even John could only speak in gulps, for they knew Hook's reputation.

"He was Blackbeard's bo'sun," John whispered. "He is the worst of them all."

"That's him," moaned Peter.

"What is he like? Is he big?" enquired John.

"He is not so big as he was," boasted Peter.

"How do you mean?"

"I cut off a bit of him."

"You!" guffawed John in disbelief.

"Yes, me," declared Peter sharply.

"I wasn't meaning to be disrespectful," apologised John.

"Oh, all right," said Peter in a forgiving tone.

"But, I say, what bit?" questioned John eagerly.

"His right hand," announced Peter.

"Then he can't fight now?"

"Oh, can't he just!"

"Left-hander?"

"He has an iron hook instead of a right hand, and he claws with it," stated Peter grimly.

- Now re-read the passage, using different synonyms. Write each of your new synonyms above the word in the text.

Dear Helper,

Objective: to collect synonyms that will be useful in writing dialogue.

Remind your child that a synonym is a word with a similar meaning to another. Help your child to identify the synonyms of 'said' in the passage and to think of new ones. Check that the new ones are appropriate as you re-read the text together, replacing the synonyms.

Name:

W

A wet blanket

- Do you know or can you guess the meanings of these common expressions? Complete the Meaning column. The first one has been done for you.
- Add any other expressions that you know and write down their meanings.

A wet blanket

a discouraging person

At a loose end

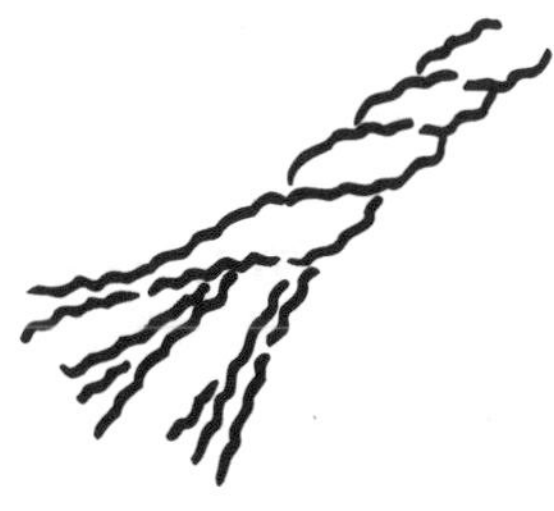

Get into hot water

Lead a dog's life

Sit on the fence

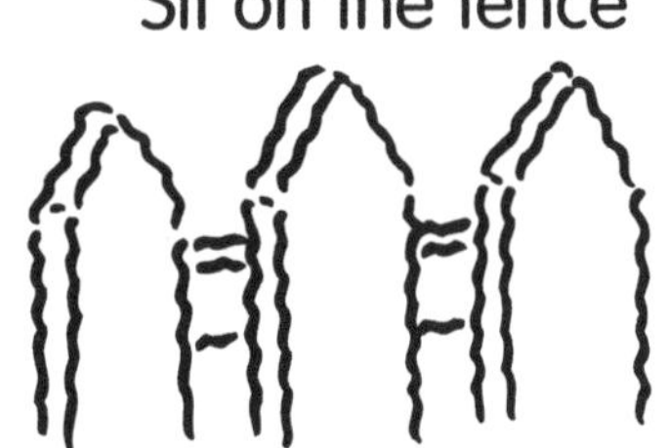

Pull a leg

Common expression	Meaning
Out of sorts	
Smell a rat	
Take forty winks	
Throw in the towel	
Add two more below:	

Dear Helper,

Objective: to investigate common expressions.

Many common expressions that are well known to adults are a mystery to children! Encourage your child to guess any meanings that they don't know before you tell them. Help them to think of and define some more.

W Name:

Provide a pronoun

- Improve the sentences below by replacing a **noun** with a **pronoun** when the noun has been repeated.

  Here is an example:

  Katie rushed into the classroom. Katie was late.
  Katie rushed into the classroom. She was late.

  These are some pronouns you can use:

  I you he she it we they me him her us them

Amra fell heavily. Amra hurt her knee.

I have a cat. I am very fond of the cat.

The magnet belongs to Tom. The magnet is very powerful.

Tim works hard at school. Tim wants to do well.

Debbie and I went to the library to get a book. Debbie and I found the book.

James is a tall boy. James is very athletic. I admire James.

The teacher praised the children. The children had worked very hard. The teacher congratulated the children.

Jane was very careless. Jane lost her purse. Luckily, on her way home, Jane found her purse.

Dear Helper,

Objective: to substitute pronouns for common and proper nouns.

Remind your child that a *pronoun* is a word used to replace a *noun* (naming word) to help reduce repetition and improve the writing. Help your child to find which nouns should be replaced and to choose the correct pronouns.

Name:

S

Roboteach

- Improve this text by choosing suitable pronouns to put in place of the words in bold. Write each pronoun in the space after the noun.

These are some personal pronouns you can use:

I you he she it we they me him her us them

These are some possessive pronouns you can use:

my mine your yours his hers its our ours their theirs

Class 3 gasped with amazement as Roboteach, the new teacher, entered the room. **Roboteach** ____________ was six feet tall and made of metal.

"Good morning, Class 3," **Roboteach** ____________ said in a harsh voice. "**Roboteach's** ____________ name is Roboteach, but **Class 3** ____________ must call me Sir."

At that moment Karen came into the room. "Good morning, Karen," said Roboteach. "**Roboteach** ____________ can see from **Roboteach's** ____________ database that **Karen** ____________ have already been late 17 times this term."

Karen went to her place and whispered to Katia: "I wish I was in Class 4. Class 4's teacher is much nicer!"

Tom couldn't help laughing. Roboteach turned towards **Tom** ____________. "As for **Tom** ____________, Tom Jenkins, **Tom's** ____________ average mark this term has been 23 per cent! **Tom** ____________ will have to work harder from now on."

Tom groaned, but **Tom's** ____________ friend Tim groaned louder. "At least it's better than **Tim's** ____________. **Tim** ____________ got 19 per cent!"

Dear Helper,

Objective: to distinguish personal pronouns from possessive pronouns.

Remind your child that *personal* pronouns stand in place of a person or thing. A *possessive* pronoun shows that someone owns or possesses something. When your child has finished, ask them to read through their version aloud to see if it sounds right. Common sense will then act as a valuable check on the choice of pronouns.

PHOTOCOPIABLE

Name:

In agreement

A **pronoun** must always have the same **person** and **number** as the **verb** it goes with.

pronoun: stands in place of a noun

verb: doing word

person: who, for example: I, you, we, they

number: singular or plural

- Rewrite these sentences so that the verb agrees with the pronoun in person and number.

1 They was always bottom of the class.

2 I is a jazz musician.

3 You is making me laugh!

4 We is going on holiday tomorrow.

5 He, with four friends, were late for school.

6 She, like Sally, are tall for her age.

7 They, with a black dog, was crossing the field.

8 Neither you nor he are to blame.

Dear Helper,

Objective: to ensure grammatical agreement of pronouns and verbs.

Help your child to correct the sentences. If your child is in doubt, get them to write out the appropriate verb table (ie 'I am, you are, he/she/it is', and so on). If they have trouble with 5, 6 or 7, help them to read the sentence without the clause within the commas.

Name:

S

Willa's baby

- Highlight all the speech marks and other dialogue punctuation in this passage.

This passage, from *Storm* by Kevin Crossley-Holland, describes the night that Willa's baby is born.

"A cup of tea first," said Annie's mother, looking pleased and shiny.

"You said Christmas," protested Annie.

"You never can tell," said her mother. "Anyhow, early or late, storm or no storm, it's on its way. There's no stopping it now!"

"You could call it Storm," said Mr Carter unexpectedly.

"That's not a name," said Annie.

"Storm?" said Willa.

"Storm," repeated Annie's mother. "That's an old name in these parts."

"Shall I ring the hospital?" said Willa. "I know there's time but..."

"I'll ring while you get yourself packed and ready," said her mother.

"Ask them to come for me in half-an-hour," said Willa and, taking her tea with her, she went back upstairs to get ready.

Extension

- Write a piece of dialogue between two people, using speech marks and other dialogue punctuation correctly.

Dear Helper,

Objective: to use speech marks and other dialogue punctuation appropriately.

Check that your child has highlighted all the dialogue punctuation. Note in particular where punctuation is placed before closing speech marks. Help your child to use the punctuation appropriately in their own writing.

Name:

Grace Darling

A **conjunction** is a joining word. It joins parts of a sentence together.

For example: Grace got in the boat **and** began to row.

Some common conjunctions are:

and if so while though since when

- Read this true story about Grace Darling. Choose one of the conjunctions above to put in each gap below. You may use each conjunction in the list only once.

On the morning of September 7, 1838, the steamer *Forfarshire* was caught in a storm ____________ she was on her way to Liverpool. She hit a rock ____________ began to sink. No other lifeboat dared to risk the storm ____________ Grace and her father, William, put to sea in a small boat. They managed to reach the wreck, ____________ they could only rescue five people in their small boat. ____________ they reached the shore, William, helped by two of the men, went to save the four others. However, ____________ Grace had not been brave enough to help her father on the first trip, all nine people would have drowned. For her bravery, Grace was awarded a Gold Medal, and so many people requested locks of her hair that she joked that she had been almost bald ____________ the rescue!

Dear Helper,

Objective: to join sentences using conjunctions.

Read through this story with your child and discuss the most appropriate conjunction for each gap.

Name:

S

Time sequence

- Choose one of the words and phrases showing time sequence to fill each gap in the text below. You may use each word or phrase once only.

a long time after again first in the end not long one day when at last

__________ in 1066, Duke William landed at Hastings.	The __________ thing he did was to order his cavalry to charge.	But the English axemen held them off for __________
__________ they weakened and fled.	__________ the English saw this they ran after them.	But it was __________ before they were surrounded and killed.
__________ this disaster, the English were badly weakened.	So the Normans attacked __________.	__________ King Harold was hit in the eye by an arrow. The battle was lost.

- Think of more words that show time sequence and make a list of them.

Dear Helper,

Objective: to investigate how words and phrases can signal time sequences.

Help your child by checking that the words chosen to fill the gaps are appropriate. Help them to brainstorm more time sequence words. Try looking in books, magazines and newspapers at home.

PHOTOCOPIABLE

T

Name:

The Ant and the Grasshopper

But when the winter came, the Grasshopper found himself dying of hunger. He did not sing and dance then, he just lay still and watched the ants sharing out the food they had collected in the summer.

One fine summer's day, a Grasshopper was hopping about in a field, chirping and singing to its heart's content. After a while, an Ant struggled by, carrying a huge corn cob to his nest.

The Ant shook his head and took up his heavy load again. Backwards and forwards he went, all day, with one heavy load after another.

Then the Grasshopper knew the truth of the old saying, "It is wise to prepare for hard times."

The Grasshopper laughed at him. He waved his forelegs around and said, "There is food all around us, and winter is a long time away. Stop working, and sing and dance with me!"

"Why not come and play with me," said the Grasshopper, "instead of working so hard on such a fine day?"

"I am helping to store food for the winter," said the Ant, "and, if you were wise, you would do the same."

- This fable by Aesop has been jumbled up. Read each paragraph carefully, then cut out the paragraphs and try to put the story in the right order. When it sounds right, paste the paragraphs onto a new sheet of paper. Finally, see if you can retell the story without looking at the sheet!

Dear Helper,

Objective: to place the main points of a story in sequence.

Make sure that your child reads each paragraph carefully before cutting them up. When your child is deciding the correct order, ask them to tell you why they have chosen to place one paragraph before or after another. When they are happy with their decisions and have stuck the paragraphs down, ask them to retell the story.

Name:

T

Will-o'-the-wykes and bogles

Doctor Grant's lights were still on. His curtains were the colour of ripe peaches. And a lantern, swaying in his porch, threw a pool of soft, shifting light over the flagstones and gravel outside the front door.

Annie stared and stared as if she had never seen bright light before. In the gloom of the great storm, nothing had looked quite definite and many things looked frightening: the reaching arms of the tree, the fallen body of the milk churn, the gleam and flash of water. There was the danger, too, of meeting these chancy things that only come out at night – will-o'-the-wykes and bogles and boggarts and the black dog, Shuck... and worst of all there was the ghost.

- Read this passage from *Storm* by Kevin Crossley-Holland. How would you describe the atmosphere that is created?

- Highlight the language that helps to build up the atmosphere.

Dear Helper,

Objective: to investigate language that is used to create atmosphere in a story.
Help your child to find the right words to describe the atmosphere in the extract and to highlight or underline the words and phrases that help to create it. Discuss what might happen next.

T

Name:

First or third?

- Read these two story extracts and say which is written in the first person and which is written in the third person.

I can't tell you exactly what happened next. It was all too sudden and blurry. I heard voices, I know that. A lot of people went, "Ahhh!" as they breathed in, like the audience in a cinema watching a scary bit. Then all at once there was this loud panting and a great pounding of paws and it was as if all the sand in the sandpit was being whipped up by some wild sort of tornado. It was brilliant. Next thing I knew, Sal was flat on her back getting licked all over by the craziest looking dog you ever saw!

from *The Sniff Stories* by Ian Whybrow

Written in the _______________ person.

"Seven swans a-swimming," sang Annie, "six geese a-laying..."

Annie was walking along the edge of the marsh, in no particular hurry because it was the first day of the Christmas holidays. After a while she began to practise clicking her fingers in time with the numbers. "Three," – CLICK! – "three French hens, two," – CLICK! – "two turtle doves..."

Annie was used to being on her own. She was used to talking and singing to herself, and playing games like two-handed poohsticks and patience and solitaire. She really had no choice because her sister Willa was already grown up and married to Rod...

from *Storm* by Kevin Crossley-Holland

Written in the _______________ person.

- Think about the advantages and disadvantages of using the first or third person.

Extension

- Write two short paragraphs of stories on the back of this sheet – one in the first person and one in the third person.

Dear Helper,

Objective: to distinguish between stories written in the first and third person.

If your child is unsure about which is which, get them to write out a verb table for the verb 'to be', (ie 'I am, you are, he/she/it is', and so on). Talk about what may be the advantages and disadvantages of writing in the first and third person. Then, if appropriate, help your child to write their own story passages.

Name:

T

Stranger than fiction?

- Read this true account of the pirate Blackbeard. Highlight all the **adjectives** (describing words).
- Compare this account with pirate stories you know and highlight anything that is as good as, or stranger than, a fictional pirate story.

Blackbeard, whose real name was Edward Teach or Thatch, was one of history's cruellest pirates. The name 'Blackbeard' came from his long, coal-black beard. Before attacking a ship, he plaited his beard into small pigtails tied with coloured ribbons. He then added slow-burning matches (used to fire cannons) which made wisps of smoke curl around his face. Across his chest he wore a bandolier in which he carried six pistols. He also carried a cutlass and several daggers. He dressed in black to complete his horrifying appearance.

His ship was a captured French merchant ship which he fitted with 40 cannons and renamed *Queen Anne's Revenge*. With this ship he terrorised shipping in North Carolina, the Carribbean and the Atlantic.

In 1718, however, Governor Alexander Spotswood of Virginia sent two sloops (small warships) after Blackbeard. After a fierce fight, one of the officers, Robert Maynard, killed him. Blackbeard's head was cut off and hoisted on the ship's bowsprit. Several years later, his skull was silver plated and used as a drinking cup.

Dear Helper,

Objective: to compare a real-life adventure with fiction.

Read and discuss this account of Blackbeard with your child. Help your child to find the adjectives. Compare this real pirate with fictional pirates that your child knows, such as Long John Silver and Captain Hook.

T Name:

Pirates

- Read these descriptions of fictional pirates. Highlight the adjectives in each description. Highlight any words or phrases that show the characters' feelings and their relationships with others.

Long John Silver

(the pirate in *Treasure Island* by Robert Louis Stevenson)

I was sure he must be Long John. His left leg was cut off close by the hip, and under the left shoulder he carried a crutch, which he managed with great skill, hopping about upon it like a bird. He was very tall and strong, with a face as big as a ham – plain and pale, but intelligent and smiling. Indeed, he seemed in the most cheerful mood, whistling as he moved about among the tables, with a merry word or a slap on the shoulder for his favourite guests.

Captain Hook (the pirate in *Peter Pan* by James M Barrie)

He was carried in on a chair by his men – whom he treated like dogs. His face was corpse-like, and his hair was dressed in long curls, which looked like black candles and gave him a threatening look. His eyes were of the blue of the forget-me-not, and very sad, except when he was plunging his hook into you, when two red spots appeared in them and lit them up horribly. In dress he copied the style of King Charles II and in his mouth he had a holder of his own design which enabled him to smoke two cigars at once. But undoubtedly the grimmest part of him was his iron claw.

Dear Helper,

Objective: to discuss characters' feelings, behaviour and relationships.

Read and discuss these descriptions of fictional pirates Long John Silver and Captain Hook. Help your child to highlight the descriptive words and phrases asked for. Discuss what these extracts show about the characters.

Name:

T

Sandwich fillings

- Read this poem and talk about why it is funny. Think about another funny poem you know. How is it the same? How is it different?
- Write your own sandwich fillings poem on the back of this sheet.

Custard and sand,

Toothpaste and gravel,

Raw liver and clay,

Sawdust and candle grease,

Mousetails and mustard pickle,

Ashes and ice-cream,

Hamster bedding and vegetable oil,

Nuts, shells and ink,

Mouldy leaves and rats' ears,

Chalk dust and tree sap,

Squashed worms and washing-up liquid,

Dog food and bird seed,

Mushy banana and cement.

Anon

Extension

- Write a different kind of humorous poem or joke.

Dear Helper,

Objective: to discuss and compare forms or types of humour.

Read the poem with your child, then discuss what makes it funny. Compare it with another humorous poem your child knows. Then compare it with other kinds of humour, such as 'Knock, knock' jokes and limericks. Together, think of various ways humour is created by writers. Brainstorm ideas for another sandwich fillings poem and, if appropriate, for another kind of humorous poem or joke.

Name:

Eleanor Rigby

- Read aloud this poem, which was written as lyrics for a song. Talk with a friend or helper about what the poem is saying.

Eleanor Rigby

Eleanor Rigby,
Picks up the rice in the church where a wedding has been.
Lives in a dream.
Waits at the window,
Wearing the face that she keeps in a jar by the door.
Who is it for?

Chorus
All the lonely people,
Where do they all come from?
All the lonely people,
Where do they all belong?

Father McKenzie,
Writing the words of a sermon that no one will hear,
No one comes near.
Look at him working,
Darning his socks in the night when there's nobody there.

Chorus

Eleanor Rigby,
Died in the church and was buried along with her name.
Nobody came.
Father McKenzie,
Wiping the dirt from his hands as he walks from the grave.
No one was saved.

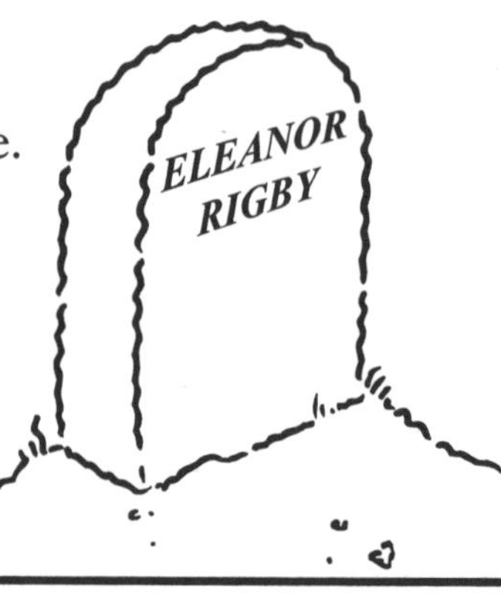

Chorus

John Lennon and Paul McCartney

Dear Helper,

Objective: to select, prepare, read aloud and recite poetry by heart.
Read and talk about this song lyric with your child. Discuss loneliness. What does it feel like? What lonely people does your child know? Learn all or part of the song by heart with your child. If you know the tune, share this with your child. Singing along to the tune will help greatly!

Name:

T

Comparing poems

- Use this grid to help you to compare two poems or songs by the same writer.

	Title	Title
Subject Say briefly what the poem is about.		
Form Describe the verse form. Does it rhyme? Does it have a refrain (chorus)?		
Language Jot down any interesting words from the poem.		
Comparison What are the main differences and similarities between the poems?		
Response Say which poem you like best and why.		

Dear Helper,

Objective: to compare and contrast works by the same writer.

Your child will have brought home two poems, ballads or song lyrics to compare. Help your child to read them and discuss the key points needed to fill in the table.

T

Name:

Robin Hood

- These cards are reminders of some of the main events in the legend of Robin Hood. Plan a new version of the legend. Choose some of these events and add new ones of your own, using the same characters and settings.

 Robin Hood is made an outlaw.	 Robin fights Little John with quarterstaffs.	 Maid Marian joins Robin Hood's band.
 Robin meets Friar Tuck.	 Robin rescues three men from hanging.	 Robin wins a silver arrow in a competition arranged by the Sheriff of Nottingham.
 Robin takes money from a rich abbot passing through Sherwood forest and gives it to the poor.	 Alan-a-Dale is captured by the Sheriff of Nottingham.	 Robin meets King Richard, who pardons him and gives him back his lands.

Dear Helper,

Objective: to plot a sequence of episodes modelled on a known story.

Discuss ideas for some completely new adventures for Robin Hood. Help your child to decide how to fit them in with some of the standard ones.

Name:

T

Sleeping Beauty

- Read this extract from *Sleeping Beauty* to remind yourself of the story, then retell part of the story in the first person (**I**) from the point of view of the Prince, Rosamond or any other character.

At last, the hundred years came to an end, and the day had come when Rosamond should be awakened. When the Prince drew near the hedge of thorns, it was changed into a hedge of beautiful large flowers that bent aside to let him pass, and then closed behind him in a thick hedge. When he reached the castle yard, he saw the horses and hunting dogs lying asleep. Even a fly on the wall was asleep. And when the Prince went indoors, the cook in the kitchen was asleep and the maid, who had a fowl on her lap ready to pluck, was asleep. In the hall, all the courtiers were lying asleep, and above them, on their thrones, slept the King and the Queen.

The Prince went further until at last he came to a tower. He went up the winding staircase and opened the door of the little room where Rosamond lay. She looked so lovely in her sleep, that he could not stop himself from kissing her. Then she woke up, opened her eyes and smiled at him.

Sample retelling from the Prince's point of view:

I looked at the sharp hedges and wondered if I dared to struggle through them. After all, so many men had lost their lives trying. Then, to my amazement, the thorns suddenly turned to flowers...

Dear Helper,

Objective: to write a character's own account of an incident in a story.

Talk about the story of Sleeping Beauty to remind your child of the main events, then help them to choose a character and an event in the story to retell. Help your child to rewrite part of the story from that character's point of view. Check that your child uses the first person consistently.

T

Name:

Improve a story

- On a separate piece of paper, rewrite this draft story by adding more detail. Use the notes to help you.
- Plan more adventures for Pegleg the pirate.

First draft of story	Notes to improve it
Pegleg the pirate got his name from his wooden leg. His ship was disguised as a merchant ship, but on deck he had 20 cannons hidden under packing cases. His crew were the fiercest pack of thieves afloat.	Describe Pegleg in more detail – make him frightening! Describe his ship in more detail – what was it called, how many masts, sails and so on? Give an example of their fierceness – for example describe a quarrel between them.
One day the lookout saw a sail on the horizon. "Sail!" he shouted. "Give chase!" said Pegleg. They soon caught up with the ship, which was a heavily laden merchant ship on its way to the American colonies. "Surrender!" said Pegleg.	Use synonyms of **said** for more dramatic effect. Describe the merchant ship in more detail.
"Never!" said the captain of the ship. He thought he could fight off the pirate because he had four cannons and his men had pistols and cutlasses. A terrible battle followed which the merchant captain lost.	Describe the captain in more detail – as a contrast to Pegleg, make him pleasant and kind. Describe the battle in much more detail – this is the most exciting point in the story. Say what happened to the brave captain.
After the battle, Pegleg decided that he would find an island and treat his men to a feast as a reward for capturing the merchant ship.	

Dear Helper,

Objective: to write a longer story.

Read through the draft story and notes with your child and discuss ways of extending the story by adding more detail. Help your child to plan more adventures for Pegleg.

Name:

T

Book review (2)

- Use this writing frame to help you write a book review for other children in your class. Make notes here, then write out the review in full on a separate sheet.

This is a review of by

The book is about

The main character is

The author describes the character as "

The book is set in

This is vividly described by the author in these words: "

The part of the book that I most enjoyed was

However, I did not like

My overall opinion of the book is

Dear Helper,

Objective: to write a book review for a specified audience.

Your child will have brought home a book to review (or notes on a book). Help your child to think about what to put in each paragraph and then to build up the prompts into continuous prose.

Name:

Moths and Moonshine

Alliteration is often used in poetry and advertisements as a special effect. It occurs when words close together begin with the same sound:

Sing a **S**ong of **S**ixpence...

Budget **b**rown **b**read **b**eats the **b**lues!

- Read the this poem, then highlight all the letters that alliterate.

Moths and Moonshine

Moths and moonshine mean to me
Magic – madness – mystery.

Witches dancing weird and wild
Mischief make for man and child.

Owls screech from woodland shades,
Moths glide through moonlit glades,

Moving in dark and secret wise
Like a plotter in disguise.

Moths and moonshine mean to me
Magic – madness – mystery.

James Reeves

- Now write your own short poem that uses alliteration.

Dear Helper,

Objective: to write poetry that uses alliteration to create effects.

Read this poem aloud with your child. You could take the verses in turn. Encourage your child to listen carefully for the effect of the alliteration and then to highlight or underline all the letter sounds that alliterate in the poem. Finally, help your child to write a short alliterative poem of their own.

Name:

Bank letter

- Read these two letters and study the different ways they are set out.
- Write a formal reply from Tommy to the manager of Bortle's Bank.

110 High Street. Felton. F22 1HS

Mr T Chong
22 South Avenue
Felton
F22 2SA
29 August 2001
Our ref: CLO 829

Dear Mr Chong

We are sorry to announce the closure of the Felton branch of Bortle's Bank. However, a short trip to Harwich will give you the benefit of a much bigger bank.

We are pleased to announce that a cashpoint machine will be placed in the High Street at Felton, next to the Supersaver supermarket.

Yours faithfully

I. Porch

Mr I Porch
Manager

---

22 South Avenue,
Felton,
F22 2SA
30 August 2001

Dear Jim,

What do you think? Our high-street bank has just closed! I'm really mad! We have to go to Harwich now and that's 30 miles away! Just think, if I draw out twenty quid, it'll cost me nearly that much in petrol!

They say there'll be a cashpoint in the High Street – but that won't help with all my other banking business. Not only that – the High Street will die without a bank. I'm going to write a really strong letter of complaint.

Best wishes,

Tommy

Dear Helper,

Objective: to read examples of letters written for different purposes.

Read through these two letters with your child, taking careful notice of the conventions of layout. Talk about the purposes of each letter. Help your child to draft Tommy's formal complaint to the bank.

T Name:

Seaside index

An **index** is a detailed alphabetical list of all the topics in a book.

People's names are written with the last name first.

Articles such as **a** and **the** are written after the main word.

When a range of pages is listed, for example **5–7**,

this is the place were the most information about a topic can be found.

- Look at the index and time yourself on the tasks below.
- Then ask your helper to ask you other, similar, questions.

- Where would you look to find about about polar bears? ____________
- In which pages would you find most information about fish? ____________
- Which page gives information about Captain Cook? ____________
- Which page gives information about the ship *The Bounty*? ____________
- Which topic does the book give most information on? ____________

Dear Helper,

Objective: to scan an index to locate information quickly and accurately.

Time your child as they scan the index to answer the questions. Ask a range of similar questions. If available, use a real reference book and time how long it takes to find each page and place.

Name:

T

Be a librarian

- Using the information on the Dewey Decimal system that you have been given, sort these books by writing the set number on each one.

Cloning and Other Issues in Biology

The Plays of William Shakespeare

Bridges

Collecting Antiques

A Social Survey of the USA

The Ancient Greeks

The Art of Ancient Egypt

Philosophical Problems

Learn French in Three Weeks

Plato's Philosophy

Buddhism

Steam Locomotives

The Chemist's Handbook

Learn German in Three Years

How to Paint in Oils

A History of Wetherby

Ancient Religions

Keats Poetic Works

Society in Britain Today

Fishing

Dear Helper,

Objective: to locate books by classification.

Help your child to classify these books. If you have a suitable collection at home, try classifying some of them.

Name:

Letter to an author

- Use this writing frame to help you write a letter to an author.

(Your address)____________________

____

____

(Date)__________________________

Dear________________,

My name is __________________________ and I am a pupil at ____. I am writing to say how much I enjoy your books.

My favourite book is __________________________. I liked it because

There are a number of questions I would like to ask you about writing. First

I am looking forward to reading more of your books, and perhaps meeting you if you should visit our school.

Yours sincerely,

PHOTOCOPIABLE

Dear Helper,

Objective: to write a letter to an author about a book.

Help your child to draft a letter to an author using the writing frame. In particular, discuss appropriate questions to ask the author.

Name:

T

John Keats

- Plan and prepare the following text to be presented as a page in a word-processed or desktop-published format.

Think about:

Which fonts will you use for headings and body text (main text)?
Will you use a different font for the poem?
How will you arrange the different bits of text on the page?
Will you include a picture?
Will you use columns?

About John Keats

John Keats was born in London, on 31 October 1795. He was educated at the Clarke School, Enfield, and trained to be a surgeon, but he later decided to be a poet.

In 1818, his first long poem, 'Endymion', was published, but it was not very popular. He also had other problems. He was short of money and was suffering from tuberculosis which, in those days, was a very serious illness. In the autumn of 1820, he went to Italy in the hope that the climate might improve his health, but he died there on 23 Febuary 1821.

Even though he died at an early age, John Keats is remembered today as one of the finest poets of this period, which is called the 'Romantic' period.

Main poems

Endymion
Isabella, or The Pot of Basil
The Eve of Saint Agnes
La Belle Dame sans Merci
Ode to a Nightingale
Ode to Autumn
Lamia
Hyperio

Extract from a poem:

There's Barton, rich
With dyke and ditch,
And a hedge for the thrush to live in,
And the hollow tree,
For the buzzing bee,
And a bank for the wasp to hive in.

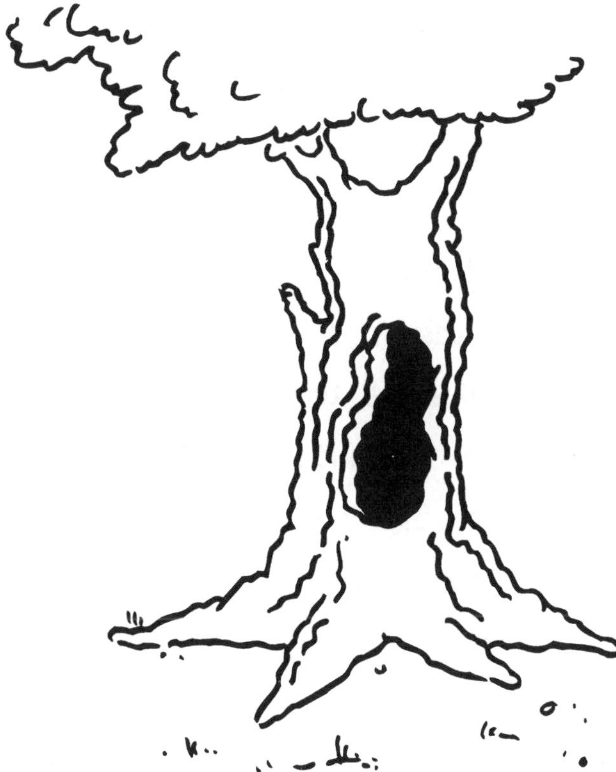

Dear Helper,

Objective: to prepare a page of text to be presented using a computer.

Read through the instructions, guidance and text with your child. Then discuss layout possibilities. Help your child to mark up (or 'annotate') the sheet with their ideas. Encourage them to use another sheet of paper to plan the layout.

T

Name:

Guy Fawkes

- Read the story of Guy Fawkes below, then think about other ways in which the story of his life could be told. One idea is given underneath the story.

Guy Fawkes was born in York in 1570 to Protestant parents. However, he became a Catholic after his father died and his mother married a Catholic. As a young man, Guy left England to fight for the Spanish army. By all accounts, he was a brave and well-respected soldier.

In 1603 James I succeeded Elizabeth I to the throne of England. Many Catholics hoped that the new king would treat Catholics better than Elizabeth had done. However, this was not to be. So a group of Catholics invited Guy Fawkes to join them in a plot to kill the king.

The plan was to blow up the Houses of Parliament while the king was there. Guy Fawkes was given the task of looking after the gunpowder stored in the cellar, and lighting the fuse when the signal was given on 5 November 1605. However, there was a tip-off and Guy Fawkes was arrested before any damage was done.

At first Guy Fawkes refused to co-operate with the authorities, but when he was tortured, he confessed. He was tried and executed in January 1606.

This story could be told in other ways, for example in a series of letters to a friend:

My dear friend and fellow Catholic,

Although I am most sad to be away from my dear mother in York, I have decided to leave England. Life is not easy in this country for Catholics and, besides, at my age it is time to be independent. I will join the Spanish army – and return, perhaps when someone more favourable to Catholics comes to the throne.

- What do you think the next letters would say? Write one or two on a separate sheet.
- Write a list of other ways in which the story of Guy Fawkes could be told.

PHOTOCOPIABLE

Dear Helper,

Objective: to experiment with telling the same event in a variety of ways.

Read the story of Guy Fawkes with your child and help them to write another letter. Discuss other ways, besides through letters, that the story could be presented, eg as a newspaper report, as a ballad and so on.

Name:

T

Letters

Here are some guidelines about paragraphs you should remember when you are writing letters:

Start a new paragraph for each new topic.

Handwritten letters usually indicate a new paragraph by indenting the first line (by about 1 cm). There are not whole blank lines between paragraphs.

Printed letters often use block paragraphs. Block paragraphs show a new paragraph by leaving a whole blank line. There are no indentations.

- Organise this letter into paragraphs. Write it out on a separate piece of paper.

Dear Tom,

We are settling in well in our new house. I miss our old house, but I really like my new bedroom. It is much bigger than the old one, so there's plenty of space for my toy soldiers. My sister has been moaning because she says that my bedroom is bigger than hers. This is true, but she's got the best view. By the way, did I leave this month's 'Wargame' magazine at your house? I've looked for it everywhere and I can't find it. I want it because there's a great Zargian battle tank that I want to buy which was in the advertisements. The best news of all is that my dad says that you can come and stay in the summer holidays. We'll have a great time! Bring all your toy soldiers and we'll have a battle. I bet I'll win, 'cause I'll have my new battle tank by then!

See you soon,

Tim

Extension

- Write a short letter to a friend in paragraphs.

Dear Helper,

Objective: to organise a letter into simple paragraphs.

Read the guidelines with your child, ensuring they understand them. Then check to see if they apply them correctly in rewriting the letter. If appropriate, encourage your child to write a letter to a friend.

Name:

Book organisation

- This is a page plan (flat plan) for a book on the solar system. Write a contents and index page for the book.

The Solar System	Contents page 1
The Sun page 2	Mercury page 3
Venus page 4	Earth page 5
Mars page 6	Asteroids page 7
Jupiter page 8	Saturn page 9
Uranus page 10	Neptune page 11
Plato page 12	Comets page 13
Glossary page 14	Index page 15

- Reorganise the chapters in alphabetical order, and write new contents and index pages.

Dear Helper,

Objective: to make alphabetically ordered texts.
Help your child to experiment with different ways of organising the information in this book.

Name:

T

Crabs

- Read this passage about crabs. Highlight five facts that you think are important. Then rewrite your five facts in one paragraph.

Crabs are related to lobsters and shrimps. Thy have five pairs of legs, the first pair having claws. The other four pairs are used for walking, which most crabs do by moving sideways. Most crabs have hard shells, though the Hermit Crab does not grow a shell of its own. It has to find one on the sea-bed.

Crabs come in all sizes. The smallest are Pea Crabs, which are like tiny insects. The largest are Japanese Spider Crabs, which may measure up to 3.5 metres from tip to tip of their outstretched claws.

Some types of crab eat vegetables and some catch live animals, but most crabs find their food by scavenging, in other words by searching around for scraps of dead or decaying matter.

Crabs lay eggs, and their young have to shed their shell every time they get larger and grow a new one. Crabs live between 3 and 12 years.

Objective: to summarise in writing the content of a passage or text.

The hardest part is deciding which five facts to choose. Help your child to choose five of the most important that are well spread out through the passage.

Year 3 Homework Diary

Name ______________________

Name of activity	**Date sent home**	**Child's comments**		**Helper's comments**	**Teacher's comments**
		Did you like this? ☑ Tick a face.	**Write some comments on what you learned.**		
		☺ a lot 😐 a little ☹ not much			
		☺ a lot 😐 a little ☹ not much			
		☺ a lot 😐 a little ☹ not much			
		☺ a lot 😐 a little ☹ not much			